FIGHTING WORDS

In-Depth Interviews with the
Biggest Names in Mixed Martial Arts

Mike Straka

HDNet

TRIUMPH
BOOKS

TRIUMPHBOOKS.COM

Library of Congress Cataloging-in-Publication Data

Straka, Mike.
  Fighting words : in-depth interviews with the biggest names in mixed martial arts / Mike Straka.
     p. cm.
  ISBN 978-1-60078-563-4
  1. Martial arts. 2. Martial artists—Interviews. I. Title.
  GV1112.S75 2011
  796.6—dc22
                    2011005591

This book is available in quantity at special discounts for your group or organization. For further information, contact:

Triumph Books
542 South Dearborn Street
Suite 750
Chicago, Illinois 60605
(312) 939–3330
Fax (312) 663–3557
www.triumphbooks.com

Printed in U.S.A.

ISBN: 978-1-60078-563-4

Cover design by Paul Petrowsky

Interior design by Amy Carter

Photos courtesy of AP Images (Pages 1, 29, 57, 99, 125, 141, 181, and 209) & Getty Images (Pages 15, 45, 71, 87, 111, 157, and 195)

Fighting Words with Mike Straka logo designed by Todd Mueller

This book is dedicated to my girls, Emily, Maxine, and Olive, for their unconditional love, and to the late Charles "Mask" Lewis, who took this squirrel trying to get a nut and made me feel like family, made me *believe*, and inspired me to go for it by living his own dream of making TapouT the biggest MMA clothing brand on the planet.

You were taken too soon, Mask. I miss hearing "Big Miiiiiiiike," but I still hear it in my mind and feel it in my heart. Your legacy lives on through every person wearing the TapouT logo.

CONTENTS

FOREWORD

I've known Mike Straka for several years now, dating back to the days when the UFC's biggest shows were in places like the Mohegan Sun Casino in Connecticut or Atlantic City's Boardwalk Hall.

MMA has come a long way since then, and Mike has been one of the constants in a sport that has seen its share of fair-weather friends. I first met Mike in Geraldo Rivera's office at FOX News in 2001. I had just done a spot on Geraldo's show, and Mike was doing a little web show called *FOX Fight Game*. I knew right away Mike's enthusiasm for MMA came from a sincere place, and he asked knowledgeable questions that, for those days, were unique in that they weren't the typical mainstream media questions we in the MMA world were used to getting.

Since then, MMA has blossomed into the fastest-growing sport in the world—just as Dana White predicted it would—and my career, as well as Mike's, has come a long way. These days Mike hosts *Fighting Words with Mike Straka* on Mark Cuban's HDNet. It is the only one-on-one interview show for guys like me, and this book will give you an in-depth look at what makes us cage fighters tick.

— Randy Couture

INTRODUCTION

HDNet's *Fighting Words with Mike Straka* **is the brainchild of Mark Cuban** and Andrew Simon. They wanted a no-frills interview program where fans could learn a lot more about their favorite fighters than just how they trained for their last fight or when they think they'll be ready for a title shot.

When I sit down to interview fighters, I do as much research about their fight careers and lives as possible, but I don't ever go into an interview with a stringent list of questions. To me, listening to where my guest is taking an interview is part of the process, and I always try to have a conversation, rather than a linear question-and-answer session.

When I asked Frank Shamrock how he was coping with the death of his adoptive father, Bob (also Ken Shamrock's adoptive father), Frank said he was at peace but wished he got to say some more things before he died. I could have left it at that, but I asked him what things he wished he could have said, and when he elaborated his eyes welled up with tears.

It wasn't my intention to get one of the toughest guys in the sport to cry, but it was a special moment that made for good television.

When I interviewed middleweight Chael Sonnen the day after he suffered a heartbreaking title-fight loss to Anderson Silva at UFC 117, Sonnen was not his typical full-of-bravado self. He was raw and vulnerable, and viewers who went into that interview hating the guy for his cocky persona came out of it as Sonnen fans.

In the episode with Roger Huerta—the first MMA fighter to ever be on the cover of *Sports Illustrated*—viewers saw an introspective man who was still struggling with the demons of a childhood rife with abuse. Abandoned by his parents before the age of seven, he was at one point homeless, walking the streets of El Salvador selling picture frames for money. A reunion with his father and stepmother in Texas was worse, and Huerta has told stories of the physical and mental harm he suffered at their hands.

When I interviewed Roger, one of the things that struck me as notable was that when he talked about fighting, he didn't seem very happy. During the interview it became apparent that every time he steps into the cage, he's fighting his past more than he's fighting his opponent. However, contrast that to when we talked about his fledgling acting career and studying the craft of acting with his friend, actor Mickey Rourke, and everything about Huerta livened up. His back straightened, his eyes smiled, and his voice became animated.

These are the types of revelations we strive for on *Fighting Words*, and inside these pages I've written each chapter based on an episode of the show.

This book is *not* a hard-hitting look at the sport of mixed martial arts, nor is it a history of the sport. There are several books like that out there, and my favorites are written by authors such as Jonathan Snowden, Sam Sheridan, Kelly Crigger, Loretta Hunt, Stitch Duran, Erich Krauss, and Jon Wertheim.

This is a book for fans who love MMA and who want to know more about the fighters and industry leaders who make the fastest-growing sport in the world what it is today.

I hope you enjoy it.

CHAPTER 1

DANA WHITE, UFC PRESIDENT

I admire Dana White for his fortitude, his work ethic, and his passion for mixed martial arts and the UFC brand of which he is captain. If it weren't for Dana White, people like me who make a living in the MMA industry, whether we are journalists, commentators, fighters, promoters, managers, agents, retailers, or ring girls—wouldn't be where we are today, and like it or not, we owe Dana White for that.

I've interviewed Dana more than 50 times over the past decade, but no matter how many times I do, I'm always a bit intimidated. He is after all, the Godfather of MMA, the Grand Poobah of the UFC.

The first time I interviewed Dana was in 2001 when I was the weekend sports contributor on FOX News Channel, and I think the first thing he said to me was, "I don't know if we're going to fucking make it, but I love this sport more than anything." Right there I fell in love with his honesty. Most people in his position would try to sell me a bill of goods about his company and the fledgling sport, but not Dana. He's honest and frank, and he's proven throughout the years that he has no problem telling anyone what's on his mind.

White was Chuck Liddell's and Tito Ortiz's manager before he became the president of the UFC. In 2001 he convinced his high school friends, Lorenzo and Frank Fertitta, the billionaire owners of the Nevada-based Station Casino Group, to purchase the organization for some $2 million dollars.

Today, the UFC is estimated to be worth over $2 billion. A lot of that success comes from White's brash, in-your-face style of doing business. Dana did me the honor of being my first guest on *Fighting Words*, even at a time when he was having issues with HDNet, which goes to show you what kind of a guy he is.

"People think I'm brash, I'm this and that. Listen, this is the fight game, this isn't Microsoft or McDonald's," White says. "This is the fight game, and it's blown out of proportion too, the whole bad guy image thing."

Indeed, Dana is probably one of the nicest guys when it comes to the fans. In business, however, he can be as tough as the most hardened Fortune 500 CEO.

Dana is not afraid of controversy. He speaks his mind and often takes to Twitter or YouTube with messages to fans, journalists, fighters, judges, referees, and competitors. He has single-handedly increased sales at Pinkberry frozen yogurt stores across the country by announcing UFC ticket giveaways there, in cities where events are taking place—while he enjoys his favorite Pinkberry treat: a large original with Fruity Pebbles.

"To be honest with you, the whole social network thing and Twitter is because I don't have the greatest relationship with the media all the time," he says.

"I feel I call the media out on a lot of things and the whole internet has changed the world of media. Anybody with a website is a 'journalist,' so I just don't play their games. The thing I love about Twitter and a lot of the social networking is I can talk directly to the fans. I can cut out the middleman. I can say exactly what I want to say the way I want to say it without somebody else interpreting what I said."

White has been known to call out members of the media by name when something they say or write gets under his skin, including Sherdog.com's Loretta Hunt and Jake Rossen.

He even tweeted a four-letter salvo to the *San Francisco Chronicle* when the paper's sports editors refused to cover UFC 117 in Oakland, writing:

> ❝San fran chronicle says they hate UFC and would NEVER cover the UFC and were such rude dickheads to our pr girl. Hey SFC, fuck u!!!! ...San jose mercury, oakland tribune, contra costa times, west county times, valley times and many more thanks 4 ur support! ❞

White makes no apologies for his public lashings.

"This isn't 1986 anymore, where the media can say anything they want about anybody and there's no way for you to respond, so when I see the media doing something that is wrong—or misquotes or misinformation or flat-out lying—I'm going to call them out on that. And I don't see what's so controversial about that," says White.

Whatever people may want to call it, it's working. The UFC has supplanted boxing and the WWE (World Wrestling Entertainment) as the world's biggest pay-per-view draws, and ratings for its TV productions on SpikeTV and Versus have far exceeded network executive expectations. A network television deal with ABC, CBS, NBC, or FOX is in the cards in the very near future, and even an Initial Public Offering on Wall Street is not so far-fetched.

While Dana is widely credited for taking the UFC to where it is today, he doesn't always make unilateral decisions. Majority owners Lorenzo and Frank Fertitta, the billionaire brothers who own the Stations Casino Group in Las Vegas, Nevada, and founded Zuffa, LLC (UFC's parent company) with White, have a big say in what goes on.

"There are a lot of decisions I make on my own, or Frank and Lorenzo and I will get together as a team and make decisions," he says. "The greatest thing I have is I've been in the fight game a long time. I know this business better than anyone does. Having two really smart, really open-minded businessmen as my partners is huge. Part of the reason this thing has become so big is because of the friendship and the trust that we have in each other."

White's critics like to say he was just a guy in the right place at the right time, lucky to have friends with deep pockets. But contrary to the petty jealousy of some of those critics, it takes a lot more than convincing two rich friends to invest in a controversial company and concept to get to where he is today. After all, the Fertittas have a lot of friends. How many of them are multimillionaires after going into business with them?

Dana laughs when I ask him if he got lucky knowing the Fertitta brothers.

"The timing and everything lined up perfectly, but people think Frank and Lorenzo and I had been hanging together for 15 years," he says. "What people don't know is Lorenzo and I hadn't seen each other for 10 years, until we bumped into each other at a wedding. Timing is everything, and anyone who knows me knows that I've put the work and dedication and time into this thing, but yeah, I've been very lucky, I wouldn't disagree with that, you know."

Before White "got lucky," he was offered a position to run another mixed martial arts promotion, the World Fighting Alliance, a rival Las Vegas promotion that had fighters such as Quinton "Rampage" Jackson, Matt Lindland, and Ricco Rodriguez on its roster. I ask Dana if the UFC and the sport of mixed martial arts would be where it is today if he had taken that job.

"I don't think so," says White. "Like I said, it was a combination of me and the Fertittas that made this what it is today. Listen, I knew the fight business, but the reality is the Fertittas are big businessmen. Back when we started the UFC, I ran some gyms dealing with hundreds of thousands of dollars. We deal with billions of dollars now, and that is the Fertittas' area. They are aggressive, smart, big thinkers. I knew the fight game, but like I said, this awesome relationship that we've had together is one of the big reasons that MMA is where it is today and why the UFC is where it is today."

It wasn't always easy, even for the Ferttitas, especially in the early days of their UFC ownership. There was a lot of opposition within the Station Casino business that looked at the UFC as nothing more than a money-wasting distraction. That's why it was a big day in June 2008 for Dana when Lorenzo stepped down from his position as president of Station Casinos to become CEO of the UFC.

"When you look at it from my point of view, Station Casinos is the reason the UFC exists today. These guys made a lot of money through Station, and through Station they were able to fund the UFC. The UFC was the red-headed stepchild of the Fertitta business family. Everybody who worked with them and around them said, 'You're going to lose your money. This is insane. I don't know why you're doing this.' But they believed in it and they believed in me. And when the day came that Lorenzo was going to leave that business and come full time with us, that was a big day for me. It meant a lot to me because I felt I was key to getting us to where it [the league] was, for him to leave to come over and join us. I knew what he was going to bring to the table when he came. If you look at what he's done internationally in the last year, he's kicked some serious ass."

Indeed, during 2010 Lorenzo was able to sell 10 percent of the UFC to Flash Entertainment, a government-owned concert and events promotion in Abu Dhabi, for an estimated $120 million. The brothers and White diluted their own shares to make room for their new partners, and the UFC would go on to present UFC 112 on Yas Island in Abu Dhabi.

In August 2010, the UFC announced the hiring of Mark Fischer, a 12-year NBA executive who built NBA China into a $2 billion enterprise, to head a UFC operation in Asia.

"I think as successful as the NBA was there, I think we can do just as much with the UFC," Fischer said, telling me later the potential big areas for expansion include China, Japan, Korea, and Hong Kong.

The Zuffa-era UFC's biggest foray into Europe was in April 2007, at UFC 70: Nations Collide, in London's O2 Arena. The promotion spent millions of dollars announcing its presence to the British MMA fans, however, much of that money was not recouped after dismal pay-per-view buys. MMA bloggers made much of the fact that the

UFC spent more money marketing that fight than it brought in for the event.

White, however, says the marketing spend was worth every penny, despite the short-term losses.

"I believed in it," he says. "I knew. Just like when we started this thing back in 2001. I knew England was going to be big. And the reason we got crushed over there is because I spent so much money. I went over there guns a blazing, especially with the marketing.

"When we put on that fight in London, I don't care if you lived in some small cow town, you knew the UFC was coming to England, that's how big I went on the marketing. You know, when you look back you're like, 'God, we spent this much money, we lost this much money.' But you never know, had I not done that, would it be where it is today? Would it have grown throughout Europe the way that it has, who knows? Now that it's all worked you don't know if it was the right answer or the wrong answer."

In 2006, prior to the first season of *The Ultimate Fighter (TUF)* reality show on SpikeTV, the Fertitta brothers were [$30] million in the red with the UFC. White was tasked with finding a buyer for the promotion.

> **"**I thought it was over," says Dana. "Lorenzo called and said, 'I can't keep pumping money into this thing, get out on the streets and see what you can get for it.' That day I was making calls all day finding out how much we could sell it for. And by the end of the night it was anywhere between $4–6 million, and I called him and gave him the number. And he said, 'All right, I'll call you in the morning.' And he called me back the next day and said, 'Fuck it, let's keep going.'**"**

While he was relieved the UFC would get an extension, the pressure was certainly on White to perform, and he was already eating, sleeping, and breathing UFC. White had some dark days during that time.

"I never said, 'I'm in over my head. I was just like, that was a close one, this thing is about to be over. You know, I was working as hard as somebody could work, but I said, I've got to step it up even more and put this thing into overdrive."

If the fiduciary success of the UFC isn't enough to prove that that overdrive worked, in 2010 White was awarded an extremely prestigious honor, the inaugural PromaxBDA "Game Changer" Sports Marketing Award.

The award recognizes an innovator who's transformed the business of sports media and sports-media marketing through the development of new technologies, applications, business models, and industries.

PromaxBDA is a worldwide organization consisting of over 3,000 companies in 70 countries, dedicated to the development of the entertainment industry. Among the panel voting for the Game Changer Award were execs from ESPN, HBO, and HDNet's Mark Cuban (my boss).

"In selecting a recipient for our inaugural Game Changer Award, we felt Dana White perfectly embodies the type of sports-marketing figure worthy of setting precedent for this honor," PromaxBDA president Jonathan Block-Verk stated. "Shift in perception, evolution of the UFC brand, and its meteoric rise under his watch perfectly exemplify what it means to be a game changer in the sports-marketing arena."

White was born in Manchester, Connecticut, and grew up back and forth between Las Vegas, Nevada, and Levant, Maine. His parents were divorced and his mother raised him alone as best as she could. Dana was street smart from a very young age, and although he attended University of Massachusetts Boston, he dropped out to start his own business: Dana White Enterprises, a boxing instruction company that eventually led to managing two unknown mixed martial arts fighters named Tito Ortiz and Chuck Liddell.

Dana's humble beginnings keep him grounded even as he hobnobs with the world's biggest celebrities and richest business moguls.

"I treat everybody the same, whether you're a media mogul or just one of the fans," says White. "Everybody's the same to me. I've always—this might be funny to people, but I've been a people person my whole life and I deal well with people. If you choose not to deal well with me, then I don't deal well with you. Either way, I know how to deal with people."

To Dana, loyalty means everything. Most of the people who started at the UFC with White in 2001 are still with him today.

"I believe that we all have to pick a team and go with it, man," he says. "You know, these people that hop from place to place looking for more money or looking for this or looking for that...I sat down a group of fighters and a group of employees. And I talked to everybody one-on-one and said, 'Here is my vision. Here is where I want to take this. Are you with me or not?' And the people that were still are, and I guarantee they don't regret a minute of it. They have made a lot of money and they get to travel the world and have fun."

Indeed, since that day the UFC has been to Dublin, Ireland; London, Manchester, Newcastle, and Birmingham in England; Cologne and Oberhausen in Germany; Abu Dhabi in the United Arab Emirates; Montreal and Vancouver in Canada; and Sydney, Australia, to say nothing of the dozens of U.S. cities the UFC has graced, from Portland, Oregon, to Newark, New Jersey.

Dana has had some pretty public disputes with some of the fighters on his roster, most notably Tito Ortiz and Randy Couture. Both fighters were not happy with the terms of their contracts and essentially held out for more money. In Ortiz's case, the feud became extremely personal, with White and Ortiz actually setting up a boxing match inside the Octagon.

That fight never happened, but it emphasized how much the two hated one another during that time. With Couture, the matter was mostly business, with White putting most of the blame for Couture's unhappiness on Couture's new Hollywood agents, describing one as "that Hollywood scumbag lawyer."

Eventually Couture gave in, as court after court sided with the UFC. He did come away from it, however, with the best contract of his fight career. Ortiz also finally buried the hatchet with White, and he, too, came out with a much larger contract than he'd ever had before, but perhaps that was more a sign of the times than it was rewarding the squeaky wheel. One of the most gratifying things I've ever seen was on *The Ultimate Fighter: Team Liddell vs. Team Ortiz,* in the episode where Dana fires Tito from the show after Tito announces he won't be fighting Chuck after all, due to a neck injury. Ortiz looked like a deer in the headlights as White explained to him he was sending him away to get checked out by "one of the best doctors in sports orthopedics."

In contrast, the UFC's highest-paid fighters have mostly been the good soldiers, such as Matt Hughes and Chuck Liddell, both of whom White considers friends.

"There's a story about me and Matt Hughes," says White. "We didn't get along too well in the beginning, you know I always got this weird vibe from him, he was always…I don't know, I can't really explain it or put my finger on it. But one day we were down promoting his fight in Miami [in 2003] when he fought Sean Sherk, and I grabbed him and said, 'Let's go for a walk.' We walked down the street in Miami and talked, and I basically gave him that [vision] talk. Since that night Matt Hughes and I have been great. I trust him, he trusts me, and I've done everything I've ever said I would do and he has done everything he ever said he would do. You know, there was a time back in the crazy days when everybody was coming at us and Hughes was the top guy in the world. He'd be on his last fight of his deal and would fight it and I wouldn't sweat it one bit. I wasn't worried that Matt wouldn't re-sign with us, and Matt never sweated me stepping up to the plate and doing what I should have done without him going out and getting five to six different bids on his services."

Contrary to his bombastic public persona, those who know White describe him as one of the coolest guys they know. When he's generous, he's generous. But when one chooses to go to war with him, he won't hesitate to bring out the big guns.

"I'm a dream-maker man. I love it," he says. "I love taking people in and turning people into stars and changing people's lives and even with the fans, you know? I get tons of emails and these are some hard times. People are in hard times right now. And I love doing fun exciting things that make people either happy at the moment or changes people's lives. You know, crushing isn't fun. But I will crush too, if you put me in that position."

Some of those people that White has gone to war with are the ones who run network television. White famously battled with Showtime Sports executives while trying to secure a television deal there, and when Showtime ultimately went with EliteXC and Strikeforce (after Strikeforce acquired EliteXC assets), White went public with his feelings in an interview with MMAFighting.com's Mike Chiappetta in September 2009.

"These guys are the most arrogant, cocky, pompous jackasses I've ever met in my whole life," he said.

When the News Corp owned MyNetworkTV (formerly UPN) went with the fledgling International Fight League—a team-based promotion run by comic book impresario Gareb Shamus, White was said to have thrown a boardroom chair inside the News Corp headquarters.

Talks also broke down with HBO in 2008; however the door seems to still be open for future negotiations on both sides.

The UFC makes a lot of money on pay-per-view, but White concedes a network television deal is good for business.

"Do we need it? No," he says. "But, if we get it, I think it takes things to a different level. But yeah, as you can tell, I'm in no rush. Listen, this company is not going to be disrespected anymore. We are not going to just jump on some goofy television deal just because some big network thinks we need them, because we don't. And we are going to take our time and do this thing the right way. We have seen all these small, worthless promotions get a network deal before we did, and what did it do to them? It destroyed them."

Indeed, EliteXC and IFL (International Fight League) were both off the air and out of business before making any sort of impact on the MMA landscape, save for introducing Kimbo Slice to even more of the masses. Kimbo was cut from the UFC after just one loss in the promotion. He got there after competing on *The Ultimate Fighter*, losing to "Big Country" Roy Nelson (an IFL champion), and then beating Houston Alexander in a bizarre match at the *TUF* finale, before finally taking a loss to Matt Mitrione on his first PPV. Slice is said to be considering a boxing career next.

White's opposed to what he describes as freak shows, where promotions use notorious or simply famous people to stunt-cast a show. When Kimbo debuted with EliteXC, promoter Gary Shaw put the entire marketing budget behind Slice, because he was an internet sensation as a Miami-based backyard brawler. Sure, Kimbo was an interesting figure, but a professional fighter he was not. Even more confusing about Shaw's decision to promote Slice so heavily was the fact that he had actual MMA fighters on his roster. Guys such as Scott Smith, Robbie Lawler, Brett Rogers, and the women's phenom, Gina Carano.

When Dana agreed to allow Slice into the UFC, it was on the condition that he take the *TUF* route, like all other unproven fighters out there. Kimbo did, and he earned the respect of the MMA faithful, if only for a short time.

Another one-hit wonder, so to speak, was the August 2010 fight featuring boxer James "Lights Out" Toney vs. Randy Couture. This fight was billed as UFC vs. Boxing, and Couture made quick work of Toney after a low, single leg takedown (a basic wrestling move no MMA fighter would actually be taken down with), leading to some ground and pound until Toney finally submitted to Couture with a head and arms choke.

Toney was paid a reported $500,000 for his short-lived MMA career.

Before Toney and Slice, however, came WWE crossover Brock Lesnar, who would go on to become the UFC Heavyweight Champion. Lesnar put the time in, training extensively in mixed martial arts before making his UFC debut. White famously told Lesnar, "the UFC is not the place to learn how to fight."

As it turned out, Lesnar didn't need much time to learn, and he proved beyond a doubt, after beating Heath Herring, Frank Mir, and then submitting Shane Carwin, that he did indeed belong in the UFC. He was the undisputed champion.

But at UFC 100, one of the company's—and White's—shining moments, Lesnar dissed a major sponsor in his postfight interview with Joe Rogan.

"I'm going to have a Coors Light, because Bud Light sucks," he said. Bud Light had spent tens of millions of dollars on a UFC sponsorship, one of White's biggest achievements at the helm of the company.

Lesnar went on to say that he was going to go home and "lay on his wife."

It isn't one of White's favorite memories.

"UFC 100 was bigger than I thought it would be," he says. "It took on a life of its own, it was crazy how this thing just...by UFC 92 people were talking to me about 100. And you know, I'm focused on 92 and 93, not 100. It was just another show for me, but it ended up being so big. Everything went by so fast I didn't really have time to kick back and enjoy it and take it all in. But the aftermath of it was amazing. And that night, it's not that I was so pissed at Brock, I was blown away. I was in shock. And I was just, I couldn't understand why he would do that to me."

I asked Dana if he felt like Brock kicked him in the teeth.

> **“**No, no when it was all said and done—I mean, Brock is crazy, you know what I mean? He's a big madman, he's a big mountain man, madman, that's what he is. And he's a passionate guy too. He loves to compete and he got out there and he got crazy. **”**

"He beat Frank Mir, he wanted that thing so bad and he went crazy after, and I tell guys all the time, if you swear on TV you are really going to stick it to me because it's the worst thing you can do. But it's going to happen sometimes, you know, and it's not like these guys are going out to directly try to hurt me and I don't think Brock was either. Brock just went a little crazy. It happen sometimes."

For his part, Lesnar followed up that bizarre and embarrassing postfight speech with a more contrite and honorable one after defending his belt against Carwin.

"I come before you a more humbled champion," he said. Lesnar had suffered a life-threatening case of diverticulitis in the months after UFC 100, and he was told he'd likely never fight again. He did. And he won, which is actually the epitome of any UFC fighter or executive or staffer at the organization. It's that die-hard attitude, handed down from the president, that fuels what has become the fastest growing sport in the world.

And while it's hard to imagine the UFC without White, he says he'll retire someday.

"People all tell me no, there's no way you could do it, there's no way, but yeah I can see me doing it. Trust me," he says. "I know what my job is over the next 10 years. I know what my job is, and I know what I have to accomplish and what I have to get done. Everybody thinks I can't do it, meaning couldn't step away, couldn't retire. Once I set it in my mind to do something, trust me, I will figure out something else to do."

And in spite of all the success White's achieved in the sporting world, in spite of all the money he's made for himself and his partners and his employees, White says his greatest accomplishment is something much more simple, yet at once much more complicated.

"I love what I do. I get up every day and can't wait to get to work, can't wait to win, can't wait to keep growing this thing, but at the end of the day, it's all about my kids. I love spending time with my kids and hanging out with them. As much as I work, as much as I travel, I try to spend as much time with my kids as I can."

CHAPTER 2

FRANKIE EDGAR, UFC FIGHTER

In every sport there are moments that define greatness and make legends. For UFC Lightweight Champion Frankie Edgar, that moment came on January 1, 2011, at UFC 125 Resolution at the MGM Grand Garden Arena.

Edgar was defending his title for just the second time, and standing across the Octagon was the only man to ever beat him, the undefeated Gray Maynard. Edgar looked at this fight as not only a chance to defend the belt he took away from UFC legend BJ Penn, but also a chance to avenge the only loss of his career. "I'm 13 and Gray Maynard," Edgar said in the prefight buildup.

Maynard looked at the title as his right. In his mind he had already beaten the champ in a 2008 matchup, where he took a unanimous decision with superior size and wrestling. He felt robbed that Edgar would get a title shot before him. He felt that Edgar had what should've been his.

For Maynard, UFC 125 was to be the stage on which he claimed what was rightfully his.

What transpired during that main event on New Year's Day, 2011 will go down in UFC lore as one of the greatest title fight performances in history.

Maynard dominated Edgar in the first round, rocking him with a left hook that sent the champion staggering into a diving back roll. The shot was reminiscent of the time former heavyweight champion Brock Lesnar knocked Heath Herring clear across the Octagon and into his own diving back roll with one solid punch.

The capacity crowd was on its feet as Maynard closed in on his prey and continued the onslaught, throwing a total of 97 punches during the round, each one with bad intentions.

Frankie staggered around the Octagon. He was dropped four more times. He held on to the cage for dear life, and while referee Yves Levigne warned him not to grab the fence, Maynard, in a move that looked more like street fight brawl than MMA championship bout, relentlessly dragged him back down to the canvas for more punishment.

It was only a matter of time before one of those big hands would put the champion away for good, or Levigne would step in and call an end to the bout, giving Maynard what he considered his birthright.

"I've been training for this since I [was] three years old," Maynard said repeatedly.

There was only one person who would have argued a TKO stoppage had Levigne made that call. There was only one person who believed that Frankie Edgar could not only survive that early onslaught and that amount of damage, but also fight his way back into the match and nullify Maynard's accomplishment in those first five minutes that night.

Frankie Edgar.

"There's no quit in me," he would say later that night.

The champion not only survived the round, but before the horn sounded an end to what was most likely the longest five minutes of his life, he landed a solid right across Maynard's chin and then a left hook—if not to do any damage to the man who was pursuing and trying to take his head off—then just to say, "Hey Gray, I'm still here."

It was the stuff of Hollywood.

"You never got me down, Ray. Ya hear me? Never got me down." Robert De Niro's Jake LaMotta says in *Raging Bull*.

"He's not human. He's like a piece of iron," says Ivan Drago after pounding Stallone's Rocky in *Rocky IV*.

———

Fe: the atomic symbol for iron.

In 2010, Frankie "Iron Man" Edgar had the best year of his entire career, dating all the way back to his time as a high school and collegiate wrestling standout. In April, at UFC 112, clear across the globe in Abu Dhabi, the Answer shocked the world with a five-round unanimous decision upset of the legendary BJ Penn, winning the UFC lightweight belt and realizing a dream nobody thought he'd make happen. Even after the victory, Edgar endured even more doubts as to his place in UFC history, from fans, MMA observers, and fellow fighters.

The result was so shocking that UFC president Dana White gave Penn an immediate rematch in August 2010 at UFC 118. Edgar, believing more than ever in the game plan he implemented in their first bout, added a few more techniques to his arsenal for their second meeting. He ended up dominating Penn in even more spectacular fashion the second time. In fact, more so than any other lightweight who had ever stepped into the cage against the Prodigy.

Regardless, fans and observers continued to doubt Edgar. "Styles make fights, and he's just Kryptonite to Penn," they said. "Wait until he faces Maynard. Then we'll see."

It goes to show you how hard it is for people to accept someone other than the guy they've known for years. Penn was one of the most dominant lightweight fighters ever, and beating him twice had solidified nothing. Edgar would need something else—something even more spectacular, something legendary—to win over the fans and the media.

Frankie, at 5 feet, 6 inches tall and a natural weight of about 160 pounds, had been dogged about dropping down to 145 pounds since he entered mixed martial arts. The so-called experts said he was too small for 155, what with most fighters like Penn and Maynard cutting down from upwards of 180 pounds.

But for Edgar, the doubters never really mattered, right?

"I'm okay with that," he told me for a piece I wrote for UFC.com. "Honestly, I don't even pay attention to it. I'm not in it for the respect."

Then he added, "But, it will happen eventually."

He didn't have to add that last sentence, but he did, because it does matter. It would matter to anyone, especially after twice beating the greatest lightweight fighter to ever put on a pair of fingerless MMA gloves, that people are still questioning your talent, your place, and your heart.

Edgar would get his respect, and ironically, it would be Maynard—not Penn—who would provide that chance.

On that night, January 1, 2011, in Las Vegas, Nevada, Frankie Edgar would not just survive a one-sided first round beatdown at the hands of Maynard, he would come back and win round two with a performance that had 12,688 sets of jaws dropped onto the Grand Garden Arena floor, along with a few million more at home.

From my spot in media row, cageside in the arena, I watched as UFC fighters Kenny Florian, Clay Guida (who submitted Takanori Gomi that night), Wanderlei Silva, Dominick Cruz, Anthony Pettis, Forrest Griffin, Brian Stann (who knocked out Chris Leben that night), and Stephan Bonnar stood on their feet for practically 25 minutes.

These are guys who know when something special is happening inside the Octagon. In fact, they are more cynical than the average fight fan, and their reactions alone could have told the story.

"What Frankie did on Saturday night is what legends are made of," Florian told me when I interviewed him on *Fighting Words* the next day.

After Edgar picked Maynard apart in that second round, he put an exclamation point on it with a highlight reel takedown as he lifted the much bigger Maynard off his feet, stepped, then leaped off his feet, driving the Bully into the mat with a slam so hard it echoed off the canvas and up through the rafters.

Rounds three, four, and five were so close that each judge saw them differently, and the greatest lightweight title fight in the history of mixed martial arts ended in a draw.

And while this chapter is about Frankie Edgar, I mean to take nothing away from Maynard. Most men would have broke after dishing out everything they had on an opponent, only to see him get right back up and come at you like it never happened. In addition, Gray had never fought into the "championship rounds"—the fourth and fifth—ever before. Most experts thought he'd gas out if the fight went there. He didn't.

After the judges returned scores of 48–46, 46–48, and 47–47, it was immediately apparent that Frankie Edgar and Gray Maynard would get to do this again.

Edgar appeared on *Fighting Words* after winning the belt from BJ Penn in April 2010, long before he proved to the world he wasn't a fluke by beating Penn a second time in August, and long before New Year's Day, 2011, where he proved that not only does he have the heart of a true champion, but also that he's made of iron.

I was lucky to be in a unique position as a mixed martial arts broadcaster when Edgar became the champion. Because, before he won the belt and was on top of everybody's "get" list, I made him the fight analyst on my *FOX Fight Game* show in the summer of 2009, before I joined my new home on HDNet. My proximity to the new champ and his family and fight-team put me in the right place at the right time, allowing me to write the June 2010 cover story for *FIGHT! Magazine* about Edgar. The story focused on what was then the biggest upset in all of MMA (Ferbricio Werdum would claim that honor later on in the year). I wrote about our time on Yas Island in Abu Dhabi and Frankie's triumphant return to New Jersey.

Frankie "the Answer" Edgar was born October 16, 1981, on the Jersey Shore, a place known more these days for a hit TV show about young Italian-American men and women hooking up at bars and getting into fights on the boardwalk in Seaside Heights than it is for its athletic dominance in the state of New Jersey.

Edgar attended Toms River East High School, a part of the state's Region 6 (Shore) sports teams. Region 6 included state champion football and basketball teams, as well as some of the best wrestlers in the entire country, including several UFC fighters and two-time NCAA champion Damian Hahn.

Edgar grew up with his mother, Mary, and stepfather, Frank Annese, a plumber who owns his own business in Ocean County. Frank was an accomplished wrestler at 135 pounds in his own day. Mr. Annese turned Frankie on to wrestling in third grade, and the future UFC champion learned quickly that hard work, coupled with his inherent toughness, would be the key to success. He's brought that philosophy into mixed martial arts.

Edgar's first bout was a smoker in New York City's Underground Combat League, where he head-butted his way to victory in his first ever foray into MMA.

"Yeah, I was training for like two, maybe three weeks," Edgar says. "The guy I was training with said, 'I can get you a fight in this New York Underground,' and I'm like, 'Yeah, all right I'll do it.' So he gets me a fight. I end up going and being the main event at this boxing gym in the Bronx on a Sunday afternoon. It was like 100 degrees in there in the middle of June, July, something like that, and I fought this guy."

There were no rules, no weigh-in, and no medicals—just one 15-minute round.

Edgar was accompanied by his usual entourage, which is to say his father, mother, and younger sister Gina, who incidentally has been to every single wrestling match and MMA fight her brother's ever been in since the day she was born. Fifteen of Frankie's buddies also attended what must have been a surreal experience for the future No. 1 ranked lightweight fighter in the world.

He won in less than four minutes.

Soon after, Edgar entered into bouts in local promotions such as Lou Neglia's Ring of Combat, which is run by former kickboxer Neglia, along with Ray Longo, Matt Serra's boxing coach. He also participated in Reality Fighting, where he beat future UFC star Jim Miller to take the Reality Fighting lightweight belt.

After going undefeated in five professional bouts, Edgar tried out to be a contestant on the fifth season of SpikeTV's *The Ultimate Fighter.*

"I tried out, and back then they had a grappling round and a pad work round," he says. "I think I passed both of those, and then you go and talk to the SpikeTV people, then they'd call you back if they want you to go to Vegas. I just never got the call back."

But the tryout wasn't entirely a bust.

Frankie met UFC president Dana White, and even though he said the words Edgar has become all too familiar with since he entered the fight game, he did manage to impress his future boss.

"I remember I introduced myself to Dana, and he's like, 'Uh, you're a fifty-five pounder? You look kinda small.' I'm like 'Yeah, but I'm 5 and 0, and I fought at 170 pounds once, too.' He was like, 'Yeah?' And I'm like, 'Yeah.' 'All right.' So, it was kind of funny right from the get go."

Edgar may not have gotten the call to be on the reality show, but he did get a call from Joe Silva to take a UFC fight against a guy most people were turning down, Tyson Griffin. Edgar faced Griffin at UFC 67 in Las Vegas and won a unanimous decision victory, as well as a "Fight of the Night" bonus in his UFC debut.

He would go on to win impressive fights against Mark Bocek, Spencer Fisher, and Hermes Franca, losing just once along the way, to Gray Maynard. All of the experts, including UFC matchmaker Joe Silva, said that size was the difference in that Maynard fight and encouraged Edgar to cut to 145 pounds and enter into the WEC (World Extreme Cagefighting).

Edgar steadfastly refused, and it was a fight against former lightweight champion Sean "The Muscle Shark" Sherk that turned the tide for the Answer. Edgar introduced a new and improved stand-up game and outclassed the more experienced Sherk with superior boxing, footwork, and head movement. He confused Sherk with angles and relentless movement on his way to winning a one-sided, unanimous decision victory and nearly finishing Sherk with a guillotine choke that was mercifully cut short by the bell.

The Sherk fight opened up a lot of eyes in the MMA world. I happened to be walking with Edgar at George Mason University before Ultimate Fight Night 20 when Edgar was stopped by Silva.

"You'll never hear me say go down to 145 again," he told Edgar. To Frankie, who'd grown tired of hearing it, that was music to his ears.

> ❝Well, I think in the eyes of Joe Silva and some others that say I'm a small guy," Edgar says, "[They thought] I lost to Gray Maynard [in the first fight] because he's a bigger, stronger wrestler. Sherk's a bigger, stronger wrestler too, so that was just the type of guy that they didn't think that I could beat, based upon my size. So I think that just showed that I can compete with the bigger guys.❞

So while Edgar is, in fact, one of the smallest fighters in the division, he thinks he's helping to illustrate the very reason The Ultimate Fighting Championship was created in the first place.

"You know, it is what it is," he says. "If I had the chance to cut weight and get an advantage, I mean, I would take it. I try to get every advantage that I can in this sport, but, for me it's cool that I can be a natural guy and still compete at the highest level. You know, I feel like that's what Royce Gracie came in to try to show, that the smaller guy can beat the bigger guy. That's what mixed martial arts was founded on."

A match against another much bigger, stronger wrestler named Matt Veach, in which Edgar won by rear-naked-choke submission after rocking him in the second round, put him into title contention. Subsequently, White awarded a shot against the legendary BJ Penn to the very guy whose size he questioned just three years earlier.

Penn is one of just two fighters who have ever held belts at two different weight classes (Randy Couture is the other). By the time he stood in the Octagon in the balmy desert air in Abu Dhabi at UFC 112, staring across at the bundle of nervous energy that was Frankie Edgar, Penn was on a tear in the lightweight division. In fact, hadn't lost at 155 pounds in over eight years.

In the process, Penn defeated some of the toughest contenders he'd ever faced in Joe Stevenson, Kenny Florian, Sean Sherk, and Diego

Sanchez. At just 31 years of age, Penn had already fought the greatest fighters in the world: Lyoto Machida, Matt Hughes, Georges St-Pierre, Jens Pulver, Caol Uno, Renzo Gracie, Takanori Gomi, and Matt Serra.

Nobody gave Frankie a shot, and he entered the match at +500 to Penn's -700 in the betting odds.

Edgar shocked the world by beating Penn via unanimous decision. He was in rarified air in the world of mixed martial arts.

He is characteristically humble when I ask him how his life changed after that fight, and if he found himself signing more autographs and stopping for pictures more than ever before.

"I definitely get recognized a little more," he says. "Listen, from fight to fight you always, every time you come back from a fight you do get recognized more, but it's definitely 10-or 20-fold since the last time. After Abu Dhabi, on the way home when I just got off the [Garden State] Parkway coming to my house, they had this big convoy set up with a bunch of fire trucks with sirens blazing to take me home, so that was pretty cool."

Edgar would have to prove himself all over again in an immediate rematch with Penn, and I wondered if it bothered him to have to do it all over again.

"I think that you have to prove yourself every fight. People get judged from fight to fight so differently, it's crazy. If someone has one bad performance everybody gets on him. If they have a great performance, they're the best, you know. So, you have to prove yourself every time out."

Edgar is one of the new breed of mixed martial artists who came into the sport late enough to really understand how important it is to be well-rounded. Matt Hughes has said that he was a one-dimensional wrestler when he first started out, and the fact that his strength was the difference in most of his earlier fights says a lot about the evolution of the athletes who pursue MMA.

Edgar won the belt after just 11 career fights, and just seven in the UFC. While Frankie always believed he would be a champion, did he think it would happen so soon in his career?

"I never put a number on it or a time, or anything like that," he says. "So, I feel that it was just a perfectly natural progression, you know? That from every fighter I fought, I thought I fought tougher fighters with more accomplishments, from a title contender, to a former champ, to the champ."

For Edgar, a UFC career was not something he laid in bed dreaming about while growing up. However, after working as a plumber for Annese Mechanical (his father's company), he knew that he wanted to stay competitive and pursue something that used his athleticism a little more than laying pipe.

"You know, I wrestled," Edgar says. "I didn't box or anything like that. It just wasn't out there for me in this area at the time. When I came home from college, I knew I wanted to compete. I didn't know that I was going to be a fighter—and I started [competing] a very long time ago and knew I definitely had that fighting spirit from day one, but, as far as knowing I would be fighting? I didn't know until I was pretty much doing it."

One thing he did know—and no offense to Mr. Annese—but he knew he wasn't put on Earth to be a plumber.

"No, definitely not. Busting up toilets in grade schools is not how I want to spend my days. Even after I retire, I want to stay in MMA."

Before he discovered he had a talent for mixed martial arts, Edgar thought that perhaps he'd run a wrestling camp or coach in high school or college. In fact, today Edgar is an assistant wrestling coach at Rutgers University. But he had doubts after coming just one win short of making NCAA All-American status in his senior year at Clarion University.

"Definitely being an All-American would have helped me pursue a career in coaching, but it's worked out for the best, I guess," he says, motioning toward the UFC Lightweight Belt that sat in its makeshift home on top of a console table in his dining room.

———

> **❝** I saw UFC for the first time when I was in 7ᵗʰ grade."
> "I think it was UFC 1 or 2 or whatever. And that's when I first
> realized the sport even existed. Back then, it was obviously
> a lot different than it is now. It kind of went underground
> for a while, so I kind of forgot about it. Then in college, in
> my junior or senior year, it was on TV and we started
> watching pay-per-views and stuff. Then *The Ultimate Fighter*
> came out. That's what caught my attention again and I
> said I'm definitely going to at least train in it, try it out,
> maybe do a fight, see what happens. And that's what led
> me to here. **❞**

After losing to Maynard in April 2008 in Denver, Colorado, Edgar changed his camp and became part of Team Renzo Gracie under Ricardo Almeida. He started boxing with Mark Henry and his jiu-jitsu and boxing were the difference in that Sean Sherk fight.

Leading up to the first BJ Penn fight, Edgar added Muay Thai coach Phil Nurse into the picture as well. Those three coaches, together with longtime wrestling coach Steve Rivera, strength and conditioning coach Brian Blue, and sparring and wrestling partners Chris Ligouri and Mark Lee, all became extremely tight-knit, with everyone supporting one another inside and outside the fight game.

Edgar breaks down his team's contributions. On boxing coach Henry, he sees the big brother he never had.

"The chemistry between Mark Henry and me is No. 1." There are plenty of boxing coaches that could teach you how to jab, teach you how to do this or that, but I think chemistry is one of the most important things. He's obsessive-compulsive. I wake up in the morning and I'll look at my phone. I'll have texts at three in the morning giving me instruction because he's been up watching tapes. He's nuts, you know, and it's good to have a guy like that on top of you. He doesn't let me rest for a minute. He's always challenging me, and technically, I think he comes up with some of the best game plans."

Almeida, a fellow UFC fighter who fights at welterweight, owns his own Brazilian Jiu-Jitsu academy (RABJJ) in Hamilton, New Jersey, about 40 miles west of Toms River where Edgar lives. Edgar likes having Almeida in his corner because Ricardo knows what it's like to train and compete on the world's biggest stage.

"We're going through the same experiences," Edgar says. "He knows what it's like being out from Tuesday to Saturday at a UFC fight. I know what it's like for him. We bounce ideas off each other and stuff. And for me it's just, he's a little more of a veteran so I've learned a lot from him because he's fought in the same arenas I have."

Nurse has been around the fight game a long time as well. A soft-spoken Englishman and former Muay Thai champion in his own right, Nurse owns The Wat in New York City and is a striking coach of note. He works regularly with UFC Welterweight Champion Georges St-Pierre, former light heavyweight champion Rashad Evans, and up-and-coming phenom Jon Jones as part of Greg Jackson's network of trainers.

"Phil gives me a whole other repertoire, you know," Edgar says. "He's got good tricks, good Muay Thai, clinch work. He just brings something that I've never really focused on—and his experience in the game, I mean, he corners GSP, Jon Jones, Rashad, among others. Plus he's competed himself, so his knowledge of being around the sport has definitely benefited me."

When I ask fighters what it's like for them during that five-day "fight week" stretch, it's obviously different for everybody. Some guys are focused on cutting weight. Some guys—main card fighters—have to make media appearances at open workouts and press conferences (and still cut weight), while other guys stay low key.

"For me I get there, I hang out in my room, I eat and then I work out. That's about it, not too exciting. Usually we'll catch a lot of movies. I like to run in the mornings and work out around when I think I'm going to be fighting. You learn to deal with the wait, you know?

First time out it's always a little nerve-racking but, every time you do it you get more and more comfortable. It's like anything. You know, you just get used to it."

One thing Edgar is known for is his conditioning, and a lot of people attribute that aspect of his game to the fact that he's not cutting as much weight as his opponents. While that may give his opponents a size advantage come fight night, they say Edgar will have the cardio advantage. Edgar doean't necessarily disagree. He does his strength and condition training at All Star Sports Academy in Toms River, New Jersey, with Brian Blue. Edgar says Blue is constantly dreaming up more and more innovative ways to torture him, but for Frankie, there's more to it than just what's in his gas tank.

"I think for me it is just pride," he says. "I'm a very proud person. I don't want to lose and I know if I work hard, most likely I won't lose. It's not a sure thing. There are a lot of other variables coming into play, but just in life in general, as long as you work hard, usually good things are going to happen."

———

By the time you read this book, Edgar vs. Maynard III will have already happened. As of this writing, the fight is tentatively scheduled for UFC 130, on May 28, 2011. The anticipation for the final act of the trilogy is beginning to build, and you can be sure the entire MMA world will be watching.

CHAPTER 3

FRANK SHAMROCK, MMA PIONEER

Frank Shamrock retired from mixed martial arts during a ceremony at Strikeforce: Fedor vs. Werdum on June 26, 2010, bringing an end to a fight career that spanned two decades and brought the former juvenile delinquent around the globe as one of the most celebrated mixed martial artists of all time.

Shamrock was the first MMA fighter to be considered the pound-for-pound best fighter in the world, and he's held belts in the UFC, Pancrase, and Strikeforce. He is often referred to by today's greatest MMA fighters as the first to demonstrate that being well versed in all aspects of fighting—wrestling, submissions, and stand-up—was the way of the future.

The adopted son of Bob Shamrock, a Susanville, California, man who ran a home for troubled youths (and who also adopted UFC HAll of Famer Ken Shamrock), Frank would go on to become the color commentator for Strikeforce on CBS and Showtime, and one of the most recognizable faces in all of MMA.

Frank began training in mixed martial arts with his older, adoptive brother, Ken Shamrock, out of the Lion's Den, one of the first pure MMA gyms in the country. At the time, Ken was the U.S. talent acquisition executive for Japan's Pancrase organization, and through Ken, Frank would enter the professional fight business.

He broke with the Lion's Den after Ken told him he'd never be a world champion, and he formed an alliance with K1 kickboxing star Maurice Smith, a budding MMA fighter who turned to Frank Shamrock for help in the submission game.

Frank would have epic battles in the ring and in the cage, one of which took place against UFC bad boy Tito Ortiz. The two met in UFC 22 in 1999. Shamrock was the underdog to the rising UFC star, however, he TKO'd Ortiz in the fourth round with strikes to defend the UFC light heavyweight belt he'd won two years earlier in a bout against Olympic wrestler Kevin Jackson.

While Shamrock may seem as if he was destined to become a mixed martial arts superstar, life was far from typical for the Santa Monica kid born Frank Alisio Juarez III. Born to drug-addicted and abusive parents, by age 12 he became a ward of the state and ended up in various foster homes and eventually, state prison.

He credits martial arts and Bob Shamrock for saving his life.

When Frank appeared on *Fighting Words* he was about to call a Strikeforce event in Miami, Florida, that saw the MMA debut of NFL legend Herschel Walker.

I ask what it's like now that he's straddling both sides of the fence, as a fighter and a broadcaster.

"Wow, it's a lot of stuff," he says. "When you're a fighter you're very protective. You're in your own little world because you have a very precise task you're going to do. So you really are clueless as to the organization and everything else that goes on, even just the people that get you from point A to point B. Being on the other side has really allowed me to see what type of depth is inside these productions and what it really takes to get a live broadcast off, which is just crazy."

Shamrock says that he did some time as a promoter himself but found that it was an arduous and thankless task consisting of coddling talent and "hand holding."

"I quit because it's a lot of babysitting and I'm more of the close-your-fist-and-get-it-done type of guy."

Being one of the pioneers of the sport, Shamrock has a unique perspective on the business of mixed martial arts. He's fought in Japan and in the United States, and competed in both kickboxing and mixed martial arts at the highest levels. He's been around enough promoters to recognize the good ones and the bad ones.

"The market has leveled itself out and become competitive like any industry is supposed to be. In the beginning we had a lot of gunslingers. We had a lot of fans with money [acting as promoters]. We had a lot of people that saw this as an easy way to get rich. Now they realize it's a business like everything else, and the people that have done good business and have been consistent are still here: Strikeforce, UFC, Bellator, those kinds of shows."

Shamrock is an MMA trailblazer. He began his professional fight career in 1994 against another fighter profiled in this book, Bas Rutten. He is an author and wrote the *MMA For Dummies* book for the popular yellow-covered paperback. He's been a promoter, he helped launch Strikeforce as an MMA organization, and he's a proud father and husband.

He is also a character in the *EA Sports MMA* videogame as both a commentator and a fighter, but says when he plays the game he thinks they made him look too old.

"I don't remember myself looking that old," Shamrock says. "So I was shocked by how old I looked, but at the same time I was young and fresh and very technical. So it made me feel good about it."

One of the things Shamrock didn't feel too good about was his April 2009 fight against Strikeforce Welterweight Champion Nick Diaz. Shamrock looked very old in that bout and was TKO'd in the first round by the hard hitting Cesar Gracie-trained kid from Stockton, California.

It would be Shamrock's last professional fight.

"That is honestly the only time I ever went in and couldn't perform," he says. "I've fought through injuries, it didn't matter, I always performed, always been able to do it. And that night for a number of reasons, mostly physical and some mental, I couldn't perform. It has never happened to me. Not to make any excuses, but I went in with a broken leg and a broken arm. I realized I do too much. I have a job in every area of the sport because I really love it and I believe in it and I want it to be the greatest sport in the world like it's supposed to be, but that was my wake-up call. I do too much. I have to stop and focus on what is most important to me. I didn't like that feeling."

Nick Diaz has a reputation for being a standoff-ish type of character. He scowls when he fights and he looks like he genuinely dislikes all of his opponents. But that night he showed the kind of class he is truly all about.

After knocking Shamrock down and finishing him off with a barrage of punches on the ground, he helped Shamrock off the mat saying, "Get up, you're a legend, get up," ignoring the referee's attempts to keep Frank on the ground to rest and forgoing his own celebration. The fact that Frank Shamrock commanded that kind of respect from Nick Diaz says a lot about what this man has done for the sport. It was truly a great thing to witness.

For Frank, retiring when he did gives him the opportunity to focus on his family, and to give them the security he never had growing up.

"The most important thing in the world to me is providing for my family and being a good person, and that's about it."

———

Frank Shamrock did not have a family growing up, and even though he had a falling out with his adoptive family, he was extremely grateful to Bob Shamrock for everything he did for him. Bob Shamrock passed away in January 2010 due to complications from diabetes, not long before Frank sat down for this interview. I ask him how he's coping with his loss.

"I didn't take it very well," he says. "We knew it was coming for a long time. I went up and said goodbye to him a couple years ago, because I knew that he wasn't going to recover from his last heart attack and stroke and everything. It just took a big piece of me when he died.

I didn't get to say…I said goodbye, but I didn't get to say the things that I wanted to say. That one still hurts me."

I ask Frank what he wishes he'd said and his eyes fill up with tears.

> **❝** I just wanted to tell him thank you. I never really got to say thank you. He didn't have to help me. He didn't have to do anything for me. He didn't have to adopt me. He didn't have to do it for any of the thousands of people he did it for. But you know, for me, he was the first man to ever say, 'I love you, and you're okay.' I didn't have a dad, so that meant a lot to me. That was tough. **❞**

With two children of his own, I ask if he remembers what it felt like to hear Bob give him that comfort and welcome him into his heart.

"Well, I tell them I love them all the time. Sunup, sundown, I talk to them when they're sleeping. I wake up with my daughter every morning and it's always, 'Good morning, Nicolette.' 'Morning, Daddy.' 'How'd you sleep?' 'Good.' 'I love you.' Every morning. I grew up very alone, and I grew up always needing and wanting someone to say, 'I love you.' And Bob was that first guy, and then behind him came mixed martial arts and the two of those allowed me to do amazing things.

"I was in trouble," continues Frank. "I didn't have a path. I didn't have a dad or anyone to say, 'This is how you live your life.' So, for me, Bob was the first guy to slap me over the head and say, 'Look, there are rules, and you have to abide by them.' He gave me martial arts, and that was the first thing that gave me a common goal and then a place to go do it. I tell people the gym is my church, because that's where I go to get my salvation. That's where I go to do my thing."

Shamrock then drops a bombshell.

> ❝You know, most people don't know this, but I was imprisoned before I was fighting. I came from prison and went right into fighting. I was a criminal. Really, I grew up in a broken home, addicted parents, I was abused and I was tortured. Everything you can imagine happened to me, and I found crime to be the perfect outlet. I wasn't a bad person, I didn't hurt people, but I took what I wanted and did what I wanted, because that's what was done to me. And Bob was the guy and martial arts was the thing that said, 'That doesn't work,' and 'Here's how you live your life.' A lot of people are lost, looking for a way, and whatever your way [may be], my way was martial arts.❞

Frank says he was busted for a number of things, mainly breaking and entering, selling and receiving stolen property, grand theft auto, and grand larceny. He says he wasn't a violent criminal.

"I have always been a gentle person. I never got busted for drugs. I did drugs, of course, we all did drugs, but I never got into that side of drugs, the hard drugs and the things I felt would change my mind. That always scared me, that my mind would be changed."

Shamrock says he was in jail for three and a half years, beginning at 18 years old. He said he got into three fights while there, winning all of them. "They were all because somebody tried to take something from me. That is not how I roll."

He was sentenced to a California Youth Authority prison, but he had a wife and son and he needed to be closer to them and to be able to earn money to send home, so he voluntarily transferred himself to state prison.

"I took myself to state prison when I was 18," he says. "That's strong, Mike. That's what I believe you do for your family. This is what you can do. I graduated from continuation school. I did most of my work in juvenile halls. I know there is a better way out there. It may not be getting into a cage and closing your fists, but for some people it is. For some people it's just the idea of training with other people. It's the community they need. I grew up without a family. I gave up my family—because my family sucks—and now this is my family. I've had students who came to my school and come by years later and they say, 'Wow, I never knew what we were doing or why we were doing it, but I appreciate you doing it.' That to me is worth it."

On October 4, 2009, CBS televised its second MMA event. EliteXC headliner Kimbo Slice was scheduled to face UFC Hall of Famer Ken Shamrock, Frank's adoptive brother, while Frank commentated cage-side for CBS along with Gus Johnson and Mauro Ranallo.

Just hours before the match, Ken suffered a cut to his left eye that prevented him from fighting that night, throwing the entire main event (and the broadcast) into jeopardy. Frank Shamrock volunteered to take the fight, but Kimbo and his team refused. Instead, EliteXC executive Jeremy Lappen picked a little-known light heavyweight from the untelevised undercard named Seth Petruzzelli, who had been a contestant on the second season of *The Ultimate Fighter*.

Petruzzelli, giving up more than 30 pounds to take the bout with Slice, TKO'd the former street-fighting sensation turned professional mixed martial artist in 14 seconds flat. He dropped Slice with a jab and then finished him with ground and pound on the mat.

Ranallo inexplicably and laughably called the result, "The most incredible victory in the history of mixed martial arts," and could have burst a blood vessel screaming, "Rocky! Rocky is here!" I would bet any amount of money that Mauro would take that moment back if he could. It's understandable when you're in the position he was in, having to sell a fight to what was then a new audience and having to please your bosses. I think Ranallo is secure enough now and would do it differently today if he was in the same position.

Slice, despite the loss, took in a reported $500,000 for the night, and Frank believes it was the discrepancy in pay that caused the "accidental" cut on his adoptive brother's eye.

"Here is what I honestly believe," Frank says. "I don't believe anybody who has been a professional as long as he has would put himself in a situation to allow himself to be cut. Because when there are millions and millions of dollars riding on one event, you don't take that chance. To think otherwise, to me, it's unprofessional and can only be done with malice. I think Ken was upset that he wasn't being compensated like Kimbo. And for a guy who has been there since the beginning, for a new guy to walk on two or three matches and then to literally be making twice as much money, I can see why he would be upset. That is where professionalism and the business comes in. Go out and beat him and then tell them what you want."

Frank was ready and willing to trade in his suit and microphone for a pair of shorts and gloves that night, because he thought he would need to take one for the team. He also wanted to keep the Shamrock name from being sullied on national television.

"I was ready to step into the cage," he says. "I had gear being brought to the ring and I had verbal clearance from Mondo Garcia. Up until an hour before that show I thought I was going to fight Kimbo in the main event, which was really a mind twist. It was pretty hard to shift from being scared out of my mind commentating on CBS to being scared out of my mind and fighting Kimbo. I felt at that moment somebody had to do something and I was willing to step up."

Shamrock wasn't as surprised as his broadcast partner Ranallo was, however, after what transpired inside the cage.

"I wasn't shocked. You can't mix and match like that. The level is too high and there are too many probabilities. I knew it was a car accident waiting to happen, I just didn't know where it was going to wreck. I felt bad. It was like, 'Oh man, here we go.' I knew what the result was going to be."

After Ken was forced to back out of the fight, Frank went on national television and said that Ken embarrassed the Shamrock name. I ask him if he ever talked to Ken about that night to get the real story of what went on behind the scenes.

"No. We don't talk. We are not what you call close," he says, adding that if the opportunity presented itself he would step into the cage and face him in a fight.

"Oh yes, I still want to and I'm still working on it. We have to do it before we're 60." Even though he and Ken are not on the best of terms, he said that fighting him would be something deeper than working out differences or pent-up aggression.

"For me it's different. If you were my friend I would want to fight you because that's how I would show you respect. That's how I would exchange with you. I grew up like this. For me, if you were my teacher I would show you the most amount of respect by kicking your ass, because you deserve that. That's how I roll. That's why I don't leave my house very much apparently," he adds, laughing.

Of course, that's a pipe dream. Particularly as more and more super camps put out some of the best fighters in the same division who refuse to fight their own teammates, never mind their teacher.

"I think that when real money comes along people mistake the act for everything," he says. "That is one moment. One of my closest friends is Phil Baroni and I never talked to that guy until we fought. Now I text him every day, because he and I are joined; we experienced something nobody else in this world will ever experience. He's the only guy who gets it. And that's kind of how it is for me. I don't think of it like I'm worried about this guy or I'm worried about that guy—let him beat me. Or I'll beat him. We're supposed to be warriors."

Baroni was let go from Strikeforce in 2009 and picked up by the UFC. He was cut after three losses in a row, the last one coming at UFC 125 against Brad Tavares in a preliminary bout.

"He wants to win like all of us, more than anything in this world," Frank says. "But what Phil has a lot of people don't have—he will go for it every single time. That makes it beautiful. That makes it exciting. That's why people follow him. They know I will go in there with one leg and I will do everything I can. It's probably not smart, but it's interesting. It brings them in and it's what I love to do."

Shamrock says he loves being a broadcaster but is seriously nervous every time out. I tell him to relax, that it's not rocket science or saving lives out there.

"I grew up not wanting attention placed on me," he says. "Then of course, I got into a job where all the attention was on me, and now I'm standing in front of the camera. I just battle with this thing. When I am performing physically, when I'm in [the cage], there is a realm of physical that, you know, I'm floating. No one is there. It's just me and I'm floating, doing my thing. I'm bare. It doesn't matter. When you're standing in front of the camera and you're working with an inanimate object and bring those emotions, that's challenging for me."

The irony is that Frank is saying he's actually more comfortable in the fight, when all eyes are on him and it really is all about him. However, when he's commentating, it's about the fighters. If anything, he should feel more comfortable doing the broadcasting than fighting. I tell him to look at it that way.

"I'm going to try that," he says. "I get uncomfortable and I don't know why. I'm working on it. I also don't read off the teleprompter. I do everything on the fly, because I feel what I say sounds better. But I'm getting more used to it."

Like Pat Miletich, Shamrock is working hard in his new role as MMA broadcaster, and the two of them add a lot of credibility to the broadcast. I don't believe, however, that an MMA color commentator needs to be someone who was in the cage. For instance, I think Joe Rogan is the best in the business. But guys like Jens Pulver, Randy Couture, Kenny Florian, Frank Mir, and Stephan Bonnar all have done good jobs when they've had to fill in for Rogan or when they've done WEC color in the past.

————

Our talk turns to movies, the Tiger Woods saga, and his memories of living like a rock star in a fledgling sport.

When Shamrock was growing up, movies such as *Rocky, Vision Quest, The Karate Kid,* even *Bloodsport,* were very popular. Nowadays, Hollywood can't really stand up to a UFC or Strikeforce broadcast, because fans have gotten used to seeing the real thing.

"The new action heroes are real action heroes," says Shamrock. "They can actually fight. They can actually do all that stuff that stuntmen usually do for them. I think that's the future. It's guys like Georges St-Pierre, and the director will go, 'You know, I want a backflip and then kick the guy in the back of the head,' and they go, 'All right, let's do it,' because they can. We're in that era now. The reality is so real they [consumers] want real action. I might be too old to be that guy, but he's coming. He's definitely coming."

Frank is a self-proclaimed speed reader and mentioned that he just finished reading Andre Agassi's memoir, *Open,* in which the tennis star admitted to being addicted to crystal meth. That leads to a discussion about Michael Jordan and Charles Barkley being notorious gamblers, and Tiger Woods' womanizing. Frank explains that elite athletes often achieve that status by being an all-or-nothing type of person with a belief that they are invincible.

"I think a lot of it is that feeling," Shamrock says. "I walk into my house and I have to take the trash out and straighten the laundry and vacuum the floor. I walk into an arena and there are 20,000 people chanting my name. It's just that we live in a different world. I live in a different world. I know I'm not like everybody else. Because I eat room service three times a day and all I do is work out and do these television shows and this kind of stuff. I know what I'm doing is very, very different; and those people [Jordan, Woods, et al] are on a completely different level than me, and they have millions and millions of dollars. If you really want to find out a person's nature give them unlimited amounts of cash and let them do whatever they want. Unfortunately, a lot of people—human nature is—take as much as you can and break the rules. I'm guilty of it. I'm no angel. I've been to prison and I just know that's not what I wanted. I met a girl in every city, too. I've done all that stuff. And everybody does it. But you're not supposed to do it when you grow up and have a family and become responsible.

"It's easy to get caught up in that world. I keep normal, regular people around me, and I do normal, regular things. And it's a struggle, because I don't know how to talk to people. Everybody looks at me like I'm *Frank Shamrock*. Nobody stops and asks me personal questions or how I'm doing or just hangs out. There is this other thing in front of me. I keep normal regular people around me so they know what's going on. They can tell me who's real and who's not."

Frank believes the poor economy has a lot to do with why mixed martial arts has exploded in popularity. He thinks that Americans are frustrated and need an outlet, and MMA is the sport for the here and now.

"I just think that society is moving into a new era of entertainment. Reality TV is done. This [MMA] is reality. Reality TV is over. I just think that this is the sport for the time and for the society, and I think that people flock to it because they're frustrated. You know, if you have a bad day at work you don't get to curse your boss out. I have a bad day at work and I go in and kick my boss' ass. I feel great at the end of the day. Imagine the frustration building in people. Think about it. You have a job you don't want to be at and you don't know what you're doing. I get to beat the crap out of my friends every single day. And they like it. They come back and thank you for it. I think it's different. I think society needs us now."

At 38 years old, Shamrock has braces in his mouth, and not any designer Invisaline braces, but the old fashioned silver braces that can be seen a mile away. A lot of MMA bloggers like to bust Shamrock's chops (no pun intended) about them, so I ask him why he waited so long to get his teeth straightened.

"Two reasons," he says. "I never went to a dentist when I was a kid because I became a ward of the state when I was 11. So when you're a ward of the state, dentistry is pulling teeth. So I kept as many teeth as I could throughout my career and I never messed with them because they were so solid. But as soon as I got the commentary job I realized that this is a job I can do for 30 or 40 years, and I know 30 years from now I'm not going to want to look at my old, messed up teeth. So I made an investment in my television future. And boy does it hurt, and boy do I regret it every single day for the last two and a half years. I think I'm in the home stretch, maybe about 10 months to go. A lot of people say, 'Why didn't you get the invisible ones?' It's because they're not as strong and I still wrestle and train every day. I have wonderful teeth. I just have too many because I never had anything pulled. I never had wisdom teeth taken out."

For many, Frank Shamrock is that guy with the braces on Showtime's Strikeforce cards. For people who have been following MMA since the beginning, Shamrock was the guy who battled with the likes of Bas Rutten in Pancrase, and he recalls those days fondly and shares a hilarious story about El Guapo's penchant for talking during a fight.

> ❝Bas was my first professional fight ever, so the reason why my nose looks like this is because of Bas Rutten. He kicked me with a shoe and broke the end of my nose off. But the greatest part about fighting Bas was he talks to himself and then inadvertently talks to you. So, the first time I'm fighting him I'm new, I'm green, and I'm out there going for it, and I'm working on his legs. Then all the sudden he goes, 'Oh my legs, they are so strong.' And I stopped. Then I go, 'Wait a minute. Hold on a second,' and I go back to work on him and he goes, 'They are too strong. You cannot break them.' I go, 'What is this guy?' The whole 10 minutes went like that. He had this one-sided conversation with himself. It was the weirdest thing ever. ❞

Shamrock says he developed a strong sense of sportsmanship and respect for his fellow fighters back in those days, because inevitably you were going to see the same guys, or their camps, again in the ring. He also said there was a great sense of camaraderie among fighters in those days.

"We would go out and party like the world was going to end," he says of the Pancrase days. "Then we'd show up six weeks later and do it again. It was awesome. That's one of the most awesome things about the sport. You beat the crap out of each other then hug it out. It's about respect, especially in Pancrase, where we all started. Every six weeks we'd go back and see the same guys, and you could either rip that heel off, or you could hold it and let him tap, because you know you're going to see them in six weeks and you're going to fight him and his brother and his uncle and everybody else. I really developed a sporting-type kind of feel to my game. I wouldn't break a guy's leg. If I had the chance I would hold it and if he didn't tap I would let it go. It came back to bite me when John Glover kicked the crap out of me in '97 because I wouldn't break his leg. Once I got over that and started breaking legs everything was good. But there was camaraderie, a brotherhood that was really nice. It is true what they say about nice guys finishing last. I fought John for 20 minutes—or actually 30 minutes. It was a 30-minute fight and I got tired after five minutes, because I had him in 15 holds. I realized he wasn't going to give up and I wasn't going to break his leg or his arm or his shoulder. So after five minutes he just beat the crap out of me for 25 minutes. I left there $10,000 poorer and decided I was breaking every arm, leg, and finger that gets in front of me. If I'm going to be a warrior, we are just not playing."

Dana White always says, "If you take four street corners, and on one they're playing baseball, on another they are playing basketball and on the other, street hockey. On the fourth corner, a fight breaks out. Where does the crowd go? They all go to the fight."

Shamrock agrees.

"Fighting is universal. It goes back to the core of how we got to here. We survived the fight. Everybody gets it. It doesn't need languages. Fighting is fighting."

CHAPTER 4

JON JONES,
UFC FIGHTER

Perhaps no other UFC fighter has made a bigger splash in the organization than Light Heavyweight Champion Jon Jones.

A phenomenal fighter with the longest reach in UFC history (84.5 inches), he uses those long arms to throw devastating and creative strikes with both fists and elbows. Jones exploded onto the UFC scene with a unanimous decision over Andre Gusmao at UFC 87. He then took apart veteran Stephan Bonnar at UFC 94 with superior wrestling, including a beautiful suplex throw to win his second straight unanimous decision.

Despite wins over Jake O'Brien, Brandon Vera, and a dominant performance against Matt Hamill that resulted in a disqualification loss due to illegal 12 to 6 (straight up and down) elbow strikes, it wasn't until he TKO'd former IFL light heavyweight champion Vladmir Matyushenko with relative ease that the UFC brass, namely Dana White, gave the 22-year-old the credit so many fans had been screaming for.

> ❝He's smart, good looking, and badass. He's going to make a lot of money.❞

In one of the most dominant title performances ever seen in the highly competitive light heavyweight division, where the title has changed hands six times in the last two years, Jones dismantled the legendary Pride Grand Prix winner and defending UFC champion. Jones' superior striking game decimated Rua, and referee Herb Dean called a stop to the contest at 2:37 of the third round, making Jones, at just 23 years old, the youngest champion in UFC history.

"You can do it," Jones told me after the fight. "You can make your dreams come true if you just believe in yourself," he said.

As if that wasn't enough to make Jones'—and the UFC's—day, just hours earlier Jones chased down a burglar in Patterson, New Jersey, after he and coaches Mike Winkeljohn and Greg Jackson were approached by an elderly Spanish couple who told them that a man broke their car window and made off with the woman's GPS.

Jones caught up with the perpetrator and leg swept him, meanwhile Greg Jackson jumped in and applied a rear-naked choke while Jones figure-foured the guy's legs, keeping him there until the cops arrived to arrest him. Hearing Jon tell the story, one couldn't help but notice that the kid is just 23, despite the fact that he was now the world champion at 205 pounds, a father of two, and a husband to be.

He gushed with enthusiasm.

"I was sitting in my bat cave…just kidding," he said at the post-fight press conference when Canadian analyst "Showdown Joe" Ferraro asked him to walk us through his crime fighting spree.

Dana White remarked that New York will have to legalize MMA now. "Not only do we bring a lot of revenue, but we fight crime too," he joked. "The only thing left for the kid to do tonight is deliver a baby on the way out."

What a day!

Jones was born in Rochester, New York, on July 19, 1987, and he began his professional career fighting out of Team Bomb Squad in the small upstate New York town of Cortland. Jones comes from an athletically gifted family, with an older brother, Arthur, who plays nose tackle for the Baltimore Ravens, and a younger brother named Chandler who plays defensive end for Syracuse University.

Jones' older sister Carmen died of cancer before her 18th birthday.

His father, a Pentecostal minister, was a high school and college wrestler and got his sons into the sport at a young age. Jones won the New York State wrestling championship in 2005, his senior year of high school. He then went on to attend Iowa Central Community College, where he earned an associate's degree in criminal justice and was a national junior college wrestling champion.

Jones gave up his college career and took to MMA after finding out that his girlfriend, Jessie, was pregnant with their daughter, Leah (the couple now has two daughters, Leah and Carmen).

I kidnapped Jones from the floor at the second UFC Fan Expo in June 2010 to do an interview on *Fighting Words*. I had a camera crew set up in a suite at the Mandalay Bay in Las Vegas, but it took nearly an hour to get Jones through the casino and into an elevator, due to the fact that he was swarmed by fans for pictures and autographs at every turn. I finally had to play the bad guy and yelled out that Jon was late for a very important interview, so they reluctantly let him go free. Jones is one of the nicest people you'll meet, period, and it's not in his nature to turn down a fan looking for an autograph.

He was also very modest when I asked him if his meteoric rise in the sport had made him an international celebrity by now.

"Well, my life is pretty much the same," Jones said as the cameras started rolling. "You know, at the start of all this it was starting to change just in my hometown. I was suddenly getting invited to every party and every barbecue and everything. People start telling you that you're the best and things, and you know it can get to you and affect you in a negative way. So, to prevent all of that I moved to Ithaca, New York, a really small town where most people don't know who I am or care who I am. And it works for me."

Although the sudden fame may have promoted a move to Ithaca, Jon understands and appreciates the power his UFC platform gives him.

"The most awesome part about becoming an MMA fighter—and a slightly known MMA fighter—is I get to share myself with a much broader audience, and my only message is just positivity and you know, love your brother. So, I love that. I get a chance to share positivity."

As far as having two brothers who are equally gifted in the athletics department, Jones said it's more than just the obvious genetics that make them exceptional in sports.

"Really it's a lot of hard work," he said. "You know, my brothers and I, we set a real high standard for each other. My youngest brother, I'm working right now to keep up with him. He's still in college but he's just really promising and I know he's going to do really great things. I have an older brother who plays for the Baltimore Ravens and he's doing really great things. So, we've always been really competitive, and it's a really healthy competition. We just don't allow each other to fail."

Jon said his parents were strict in their upbringing and kept them relatively sheltered in their childhoods. "They kept us in the house as kids and I was actually never allowed to spend the night at anyone's house. We were really sheltered and we just had each other, and roughing each other up made us tougher than most I guess."

While most wrestlers who enter MMA use their wrestling as a base inside the cage, part of Jones' appeal is the fact that he was a dynamic striker from the beginning. In his first fight with Gusmao he used spinning back fists, and landed a spinning elbow. He did the same against Bonnar, clipping the *TUF Season 1* runner-up with it, along with some kicks that Bonnar obviously wasn't prepared for.

During the Bonnar postfight press conference, I commented over the microphone to Jones that he looked more like Bruce Lee out there than say, Randy Couture. He laughed and mentioned that he learned a lot of those moves from watching YouTube videos of fights. I asked him if he was serious during our *Fighting Words* interview.

"A lot of it is true," he said. "Originally it was just funky moves that I was seeing like the things that make you want to rewind it and go, 'Oh, what was that?' You know? That was what drew me; spinning backfists and things like that. There's lots of video out there, and if you take it seriously enough you can learn from it. It's been great."

Aside from Shonie Carter's spinning backfist that clocked Matt Serra so many years ago, and maybe David Loiseau's spinning back kick knockout versus Charles McCarthy (still one of the UFC's favorite highlights), not too many people actually land those fancy spinning techniques inside the Octagon.

Jones explained the appeal.

"I think a lot of them are low-risk moves, and all the stars have to be in line for you to land one successfully. So I just try to always have it with me mentally. Always thinking about great times to pull it off and always shadow-boxing the moves, visualizing the moves landing and then I just go out there and lay it on the line. You know most people don't practice defending things like that so it makes it a little more likely to land."

Jon was destined to be a wrestling great. He was planning on moving on from Iowa Central to Iowa State on a full scholarship, when Jessie became pregnant. It's easy to look at where Jones is now and come to the conclusion that it's all turned out for the best, but back then, Jon says it was a very difficult time in his life.

"I was a college wrestler, national champion my freshman year at Iowa Central. I red-shirted my sophomore year to have more years of eligibility at Iowa State, and in that summer of getting ready to go to Iowa State my girlfriend said, 'Hey Jon, I'm pregnant.' And you know a lot of people looked at me like a failure at the time, and it was a really rough time for me to go from stud athlete, full scholarship to Iowa State to 'Hey, you know Jon is out of school. He got his girlfriend pregnant.' So I just kept the faith and realized that God had a plan for me and it worked out. I just kept on chugging and now today life is great. It's a wonderful story."

Many young athletes who achieve such stardom early in their careers might have crashed and burned by now. Football great Ricky Williams and boxing legend Mike Tyson come to mind. But Jones has managed to keep his head on straight, and he credits being a father for his focus.

"Being a young man and being able to travel more than ever before, it is really easy to get sidetracked and get caught up in all the hype and all the fast life. My daughters really keep me grounded. You know, I realize that if I don't make it in this sport, I'm going to let my family down, and that's just not going to happen. So yeah, my daughters are my main source of motivation. I want to make sure they have the things that I never had or never would have imagined having, really pave a future for those girls."

One would argue that Jon Jones has already "made it" in MMA, but he vehemently disagreed when I suggested the notion.

"Compared to whom?" he asked. "I have a lot of work to do. There are a lot of tough fighters out there, you know. Lot of work to do inside the Octagon, outside the Octagon. There is just so much more to learn. I'm a young man and I'm just always learning, trying to learn as if I'll live forever."

> ❝I realize that I have a lot of holes in my game. "My goal is just to be the best, and I know it's going to take a lot to be the best. I mean, there are guys whose strikes are amazing. My goal is to be a great striker in an orthodox way and as a southpaw. There are guys who I consider better wrestlers than me, still. My goal is to secure the best wrestler in the light heavyweight division. And there are certainly a lot of guys who are better at jiu-jitsu than me. So, I'm just really aware. I think being aware is really key. Knowledge is power. Just knowing how much I don't know really empowers me. So, yeah, I have a lot of work to do. My weight class is a special weight class. You know there are no champs that keep it because everyone has such great skill-sets and such different skill-sets. So I got a lot of work to do.❞

In order to develop so many diverse skill-sets, a successful fighter often seeks out trainers at different camps to fill the holes in his game. In recent years, Jones moved on from Team Bomb Squad in upstate New York, and now trains with a variety of coaches under Greg Jackson. But he still credits his first camp with putting him on the path that has led him to where he is today.

"At Team Bomb Squad we don't have a huge coaching staff or whatever, but we have a great relationship with each other and just great brothers, man. We all care about each other getting better and those guys taught me so much. They taught me so much. It was such a great program. Obviously going up to different levels you need to train with tougher competition, bigger guys and things, but Team Bomb Squad, I give them the credit for everything. They changed my life."

If Team Bomb Squad changed Jones' life, Greg Jackson mixed up his training partners to the point that Jon was no longer the toughest guy in the room. When he first switched camps, he was greeted with training partners named Rashad Evans and Keith Jardine, Georges St-Pierre, Diego Sanchez, Nate Marquardt, and Carlos Condit, not to mention the lighter-weight greats he may not spar with, but shares the mat with, such as Clay Guida and Leonard Garcia. The sheer amount of talent surrounding Jackson is ridiculous. Jones is awestruck when talking about what Greg Jackson brings to the table.

"He's such a martial artist and he's such a leader, and you know I respect him because I know that he knows what he's talking about. I know that he's done his homework on the mental side of being a coach and things. He's not a coach who's going to hold the pads for you and do the sickest combinations. He's a coach who's going to teach you how to believe in yourself. He's going to teach you how to believe like a warrior. He's going to teach you to never give up. He's going to teach you to always be in great shape, mentally and physically. He's a real role model, and not a lot of people give me that feeling of really wanting to impress them. Greg has that power to make me want to bring out the best and want to do my best and want to perform on an elite level. So that's Greg. He gives me the confidence. With Greg in my corner, I just don't see anyone beating me."

Through Jackson, Jones met Muay Thai instructor Phil Nurse, who counts champions GSP, Rashad Evans, and Frankie Edgar among his students. Nurse is another revered guru who is soft-spoken and lets his fighters' wins do all of his talking.

"He changed my striking completely," Jones said of Nurse. "He made it way more technical. He taught me how to kick properly, how to punch properly, how to bring my hands back up. But he also embraces the unpredictable styles, like the spinning back elbows and all that, tricky things that you know we do. My coaching staff is really, really solid. I also have Mike Winkeljohn, who doesn't get credit at all. He's the reason for a lot of devastating knockouts when it comes to the Jackson camp, and he's helping me learn how to use my distance. I have long limbs. I have the longest reach in UFC history, and I haven't really been using it. So he's teaching me how to use that reach. The team is awesome."

A while ago, before the Bader and Rua fights, I asked him what fight excited him the most thus far?

"It was definitely the Stephan Bonnar fight," he said. "I go from, you know, so excited to be in the UFC and fighting Andre Gusmao, but he really didn't have any crazy credentials, so it was great for me but it wasn't huge. Fighting Stephan Bonnar was gigantic. Like going from nowhere to like, 'Who is this Bones Jones kid?' Everyone's talking about how I'm going to lose the fight and that's when I really started to believe in myself. [I] really started to train on a more mental level and just *know* that I was going to win. Beating Stephan Bonnar was just gigantic. I mean, everyone knows who Stephan Bonnar is. So going from nowhere to dominating a very well-known fighter, that's when I realized, 'Okay, it's possible. I can be good at this. I can do this.' And now I don't surprise myself when I beat guys who are way better than me because I believe in my heart that I can beat anyone."

Before Jones fought Matt Hamill at the *TUF Heavyweights* Finale, where Kimbo Slice beat Houston Alexander and Frankie Edgar choked out Matt Veach, I had just finished dinner with Frankie Edgar's father-in-law Jerry Nappi, my good friend from Toms River, New Jersey. And we were standing at the bar waiting for our check when a guy recognized me as an MMA journalist and asked me how I thought Hamill would do.

Before I could answer the man, who by now had told me that he was a producer on the movie, *Hamill*, he pulled his friends over, one of whom was former Buffalo Bills quarterback Jim Kelly, also a producer on the film.

I told them to get ready to be disappointed, because Jones was going to destroy Matt.

The group literally started laughing, and then they said they'd never heard of Jon Jones. I simply said, "Well, you're going to hear of him tonight."

Sure enough, after Jones separated Hamill's shoulder with a throw he got in a mount position and began grounding and pounding Hamill so badly that Jones himself twice stopped to look at the referee (Steve Mazzagatti, see Chapter 5) to see if he was ever going to step in and stop it. Eventually, Jones would actually be disqualified for two illegal "north-south" elbow strikes that broke Hamill's nose even worse than it was already damaged. I ran into the same guys after the fight at the same bar.

"You were right," they said. One guy told me that he's been Hamill's wrestling coach since middle school, and he's never seen anyone manhandle him the way Jones did that night. Jones may have lost the fight via disqualification, but there was no doubt about who won that fight.

It was seriously difficult to watch that fight.

"It was a great learning experience," Jones said. "And you know it let me know what it feels like to be defeated in this sport. You know I've taken a loss in wrestling and I guess that's why I handled that so well. But it made me believe in my wrestling in this game even more. You know Matt Hamill is known to be physically a lot stronger than most men and one of the best wrestlers in the light heavyweight division. So to land such a devastating throw on him and dislocate his shoulder gave me a lot of confidence. You know you can throw around a very strong wrestler like Matt Hamill and it gives you more confidence against wrestlers in the future. So it was a major confidence booster, I would say, beating a guy like Matt Hamill, even though technically I lost."

What struck most observers of the sport after that fight was Jones' classy postfight behavior. He didn't cry about getting robbed or complain about Mazzagatti not stopping the fight early enough, or even the fact that Hamill was finished long before the illegal elbow strikes. He took it like a man.

"I actually had a lot of fun fighting Matt Hamill, so it was the first fight where I was really relaxed. I'm pulling the trigger. I'm setting up combos and using takedowns. I got full mount for the first time in a UFC bout. So it was just great, man. If you put it on the line, you go out there and have fun, you know, you train the hardest, you gave it all you got, then why cry over the spilt milk?"

Jones also said he was aware that the fight played out on SpikeTV, as opposed to a pay-per-view. He knew he was playing to a national audience and that his postfight behavior could affect the rest of his career.

"I was aware of how many people and kids at home were watching, and kids in my hometown. They all mean a lot to me. So I just want to be an example and lead by example. Doing classless things helps no one. It was over. I couldn't change the result. I might as well bring something positive out of it."

I always make the point that mixed martial arts has changed the landscape of martial arts in the United States, and perhaps around the globe. There used to be a time when having a black belt actually scared people away from fighting you. Nowadays, guys with traditional black belts from styles like tae kwon do or kenpo or whatever, are almost embarrassed to admit that they don't practice MMA.

In my humble opinion, a well-rounded MMA fighter, or any professional on a UFC or Strikeforce level, could take any nonprofessional fighter in any fight, anywhere.

Jones agreed.

"What makes us tough is just knowing that we can handle any situation, you know what I mean? Sometimes I get in debates with my boxing friends. They're talking about, 'Yeah, if I was to fight an MMA fighter and he tried to take me down, I'd just step back hit him with an upper cut.' I'm like, 'Man, you're not beating an MMA fighter.' You know what I mean? We're just too well-rounded. Like how do you block kicks properly, you know what I mean? How do you properly defend takedowns? We're literally the modern day gladiators. We're what people paid to see back in ancient Rome and things. And I have a lot of pride in that. Since I've started fighting I've just become so much more relaxed. I mean, I've had guys try to test me here and there or say little things here and there but it's just, you give a guy a look like, 'You don't want it, bro. You don't want to do that,' you know what I mean? I'm sure most of us live at ease and at peace knowing that you can beat half the guys in the world, definitely for me it makes me way more relaxed and way more confident."

Incidentally, Jon Jones has a Chinese tattoo on his ribs that he initially thought meant *Carmen*, his late sister's name. As it turns out, the symbols actually translate to *Peaceful Warrior*.

CHAPTER 5

BIG JOHN McCARTHY, MMA REFEREE

Big John McCarthy is the most famous referee in mixed martial arts. Once known as the Octagon's 9th side, McCarthy has reffed thousands of MMA bouts, and the signature tagline that he uses to start fights— "Let's get it on!"— was once synonymous with the UFC.

These days, while McCarthy's involvement in the UFC is much more limited than it was in the beginning when Bob Meyrowitz and Rorion Gracie were in charge, the big guy is still ubiquitous in MMA. He refs at nearly every Strikeforce event, plays commentator on Affliction's MMA cards, appears weekly on MTV's *Bully Beatdown*, and conducts MMA referee seminars and certification courses throughout North America.

Big John is one of the nicest guys you'll ever meet. He's intense, but he also knows how to relax and enjoy the place in the world he's carved out for himself.

When McCarthy worked for the Los Angeles Police Department, part of his job was teaching hand-to-hand combat to the members of the police force. During this time, McCarthy was studying Brazilian Jiu-Jitsu with none other than Rorion Gracie, the founder of the UFC, in Torrance, California, just outside of Los Angeles.

There were even rumors about Big John becoming a fighter himself, which would have been completely feasible based on his size and his experience as both a stand-up and ground fighter.

As the story goes, Big John was talked out of fighting inside the Octagon by Rorion. John, however, set the record straight on my show.

"Rorion didn't talk me out of fighting in the UFC," says McCarthy. "I was dumb. I had a friend call me and say, 'I saw this thing on TV, you would be perfect on it. There's this skinny guy who won, you would kill him.' I go, 'You talking about the UFC?' I'm like, 'No, that skinny guy, I'm with him, I'm learning from him.' I was naïve enough to think Royce won the first one and now they're going to bring someone else in to do it. I filled out the form and I'd given it to the WOW promotion, who were working the whole thing. And Rorion called me and said, 'What is this?' and I said I wanted to fight and he said, 'You can't fight, Royce is fighting.' And at that point he offered me the referee position, and thank God he did, because that was the turning point for me."

Big John meant no disrespect to Royce, the first UFC champion and younger brother of Rorion, the founder of the UFC. In fact, McCarthy says Royce himself said that his older brother, Rickson, was the best fighter in the family.

"After UFC 2, Royce actually came out in an interview and said, 'My brother Rickson is 10 times better than I am.' Everyone was like, 'Who is this Rickson guy?' But if you knew the family you knew who Rickson was, and he was the best they had. Rickson was going to be the one to fight in the UFC when it was originally called *War of the Worlds*.

So what happened to Rickson?

"He opened up his own school in the West Los Angeles area and Rorion wasn't happy about it. Because he was the guy who was putting this together to get people to come to his school, and if Rickson wasn't going to be part of his school, he wasn't going to be part of his show. Royce was at the school, that's where he worked. So that's how they took Rickson out and put Royce in, and that's how he represented the art of jiu-jitsu, and he represented the family in a very honorable way," says John, careful not to ruffle any Gracie feathers.

Perhaps there's nobody today, with the exception of UFC cutman Leon Tabbs, who has witnessed the entire evolution of the sport of mixed martial arts from such an insider's point of view.

McCarthy has a unique perspective on the evolution of mixed martial arts, because he was there, literally, from the beginning. He's seen the level of athlete improve by leaps and bounds, and the technique mature to the point where the best fighters a decade ago, even in their prime, couldn't compete with the sport's best today.

> ❝ When the sport started it was really like an infomercial, that's what it was set up to be. Rorion Gracie had worked hard at trying to get people to take a look at jiu-jitsu in the form that his family was doing it, and trying to get people to understand that it was an effective fighting form. But it just didn't have the flash of what other guys were doing, like Don "The Dragon" Wilson, with the fancy kicks and stuff. And so he [Gracie] couldn't get it out to the point where people would take him seriously. The UFC was the vehicle he used to get people to go, 'Whoa, maybe that grappling stuff does work.' It was an infomercial to start, and eventually that infomercial turned into a sport. And now it's an amazing sport with incredible athletes, and it's a completely different atmosphere. ❞

Today, mixed martial arts is everywhere, particularly in North America. However, in the early '90s there weren't academies or fight camps that taught all of the disciplines under one roof, so as you can imagine, the fighters were pretty one-dimensional.

Big John explains.

"When it started it was jiu-jitsu against karate or boxing. And that's the way it was set up. But now the guys that are good are good at everything. Now, is Georges St-Pierre as good on his feet as Floyd Mayweather? Well, he can't be. There are so many more elements for

GSP to work and train at. The style of fighters today, they're incredible athletes, but you're going to see, the skills of the future are going to far surpass the George St-Pierre's of today. I've got kids in my school who are nine and 10 years old and you watch the stuff they do and they look like a small adult. Just the combinations they throw with their hands or the submissions and the way they transition on the ground, you look and you say, 'These guys are going to be incredibly scary compared to what we were used to in the dinosaur days.'"

One of the arguments against the so-called super camps that have emerged since the sport took off is that elite fighters in the same weight division who train at the same camps won't fight each other. This is something that most fans, as well as UFC president Dana White, are against.

Some prime examples of camps whose fighters won't face each other are San Jose's American Kickboxing Academy, where UFC welterweights Jon Fitch and Josh Koscheck have vowed never to face each other in the Octagon.

Greg Jackson fighters such as Rashad Evans and Keith Jardine make the same promise (though it should be noted that Evans recently left Jackson in order to fight ex-teammate Jon Jones), as well as Team Blackhouse's Lyoto Machida and Anderson Silva.

McCarthy can see both sides of the argument. "MMA developed off schools and camps and working together, taking one system and working to create something together. So when you're asking two guys that come from the same school, who train with the same guys—the blood and sweat and tears and hard work in getting to where you are— then to have them have to fight against each other, well one of them now has to leave the school, because they're probably not going to be able to train at the same place. And if they *can* train at the same place, then if you're Greg Jackson, you have to make a choice: Do I sit in Rashad's corner or do sit in Keith's corner? You have to split from one of them and it's a hard decision. I understand where Dana White is coming from. He's got a show to put on, and if you're the best two guys out there, I want to put you together. I don't blame him either."

Because Big John McCarthy is the most famous referee in MMA history, we talk about the state of reffing in the sport, the state of judging (there were a rash of terrible decisions in 2010), and his ideas on how to make it all better.

One thing that differs from being a referee in MMA than say, being one in the NFL, is that each MMA referee is famous in his own right. Sure, NFL fans know who Ed Hochuli is, but that has more to do with his tight shirts and ripped physique more than his reffing abilities.

In MMA, every fan knows who Big John is. They know who Josh Rosenthal and Herb Dean and Dan Miragliotta and Yves Levine are, and they know Mario Yamasaki and Steve Mazzagatti. The reason these refs are so famous is that they alone can blow a fight with an early stoppage. They alone can save a fighter from a career-ending injury with a great stoppage. And they alone can keep the action moving by breaking up fighters who stall, or who choose to lay-and-pray their way to victory.

Once in a while, the ref even becomes part of the fight. Like the time Dan Miragliotta got between Paul Daley and Josh Koscheck when Daley inexplicably sucker punched Koscheck after losing a frustrating bout at UFC 113 in Montreal.

While a bad call can certainly blow a football game, with booth reviews and coaches challenges, the likelihood of that happening has become less and less common, and therein lays the difference. But just as every fighter remembers his or her losses more than they remember the wins, refs remember the times they blew it more than the times they didn't.

And believe it or not, the catchphrase that made Big John McCarthy famous ("Let's get it on!") is the one thing he wishes he could undo. "If there was one thing I could change, I would change that," he says. "And I say that because no one comes in and pays their hard earned money to watch the referee.

"The problem is, it's not about the referees. The thing I don't like is you see some guys come in and come to the middle of the ring, you've got the announcer coming up behind him with the microphone. All of the sudden it's this, 'All right gentlemen, we are here tonight in remembrance of Fairtech University,' and they start going on these rambling diatribes. It's like, 'Dude, no one is there to listen to you, you know. Shut up and start the fight.' If you want to say something about, 'Hey, protect yourselves at all times,' that's all normal stuff, 'We went over the rules,' okay. But don't start sitting there saying, 'Let's show what female MMA is all about.' They all know what's it's about. They've already bought their tickets and they are sitting there or they are watching on TV. It's not about you.

"And so the big thing I try to tell the new guys, I say, 'Hey, whatever you are going to say, start the fight, start it clean, don't make it about you so much.' And so the one thing with 'Let's get it on,' yeah, I do it all the time now, because it's what people expect. But it isn't about me, it's about the two fighters," McCarthy says, almost apologetically.

At the *TUF 12* Finale, live on SpikeTV, show runner-up Nam Phan took on veteran fighter Leonard Garcia, and Phan dominated all three rounds of the fight. Garcia was sloppy, while Phan was sharp. According to Fightmetric.com, Phan landed a total of 116 strikes to Garcia's 70, with 102 of them "significant strikes," to just 64 for Garcia. Phan landed 93 strikes to the head to Garcia's 42, 18 to the body to Garcia's 16. The only stat that Garcia was better than Phan was leg kicks, with eight to Phan's five.

In spite of the stats and what appeared to be an overwhelmingly dominant performance by Phan, Garcia won the bout via split decision, with two judges, Adaleide Byrd and Tony Weeks, awarding Garcia the victory. The decision was so egregious that UFC color commentator Joe Rogan blasted the judges for the rest of the card.

When Mauricio "Shogun" Rua fought Lyota Machida at the Staples Center at UFC 104, all three judges scored the bout 48–47 for Machida, even though most everyone else watching the fight thought Shogun won. 2010 would also see controversial decisions for Sean Sherk, Quinton "Rampage" Jackson, and Antonio Rogerio Nogueira.

Big John was diplomatic when he spoke about the poor decisions and how the judges in MMA are underqualified.

"I think a lot of the officiating is great," says McCarthy. "What's gotten me in a lot of trouble is I've said things, and what I've said is not wrong. I'm not going to change it. It's happening today. There are people who want to be associated with MMA because it's the new thing. It's big and it's getting bigger because of the UFC. Dana White and I look at things very much the same way. Dana wants people to understand what's going on in the sport so when you have a judge's decision it's the right decision. Now, there's always going to be people who say I think fighter A won or I think fighter B should have gotten the decision. You have those close ones, and you know that there are minute differences and you could have picked either guy.

"But there are people involved in officiating in MMA who have no idea what the fighters are truly doing. They don't understand that if you're judging a fight, you should understand what kind of takedown a fighter is using. Is he using a double leg? Is he using a lateral drop? Is that an *ippon seinagi*? Is that a duck under? What did he do? Who actually initiated what went on? You have to know what they did to give credit to the right person. That's the problem. When you have judges that can't sit there and go, 'I know what that is,' and understand the setups, and what is happening on the ground, you're never gonna get good judging."

While I personally believe the referees who are cageside during bouts that they're not reffing should be the judges, rather than being relegated to simply collecting judges' scorecards, other industry insiders believe the in-cage referee should be a fourth judge, adding his score to the bout each round, but McCarthy says that's impossible.

"I think the referee has enough to do and I don't think he should be judging because as a referee, let me tell you, I don't watch the fight when I'm inside the same way I watch when I'm outside. In a fight things happen and one guy may be taking more damage than the other, and then I tend to watch that guy a lot more than I watch the other guy, and that's not fair to either guy. I think the referee should do his job and the three judges should do their job.

" There's positioning when it comes to referees," he continues. "We've got referees standing people up out of position. I've got tapes, or I go to shows, and I see a fighter standing up and he's taking a beating, he's getting beat down, and he can't take this guy down and finally he gets him down and he starts working, gets to a side control, he's just taken two and a half minutes of getting his butt kicked, now he's in side control and he takes 15 seconds and boom, the referee goes, 'Stop, stand up.' And you look and you go, 'Do you understand what you're doing?' And now you've got the fighter not only fighting his opponent but also the referee. And it's unfair, it's unfortunate. I've been in there, and I see a guy take an opponent down, get into a mount position and I hear the crowd screaming, 'Stand them up!' cause they want to see that huge knockout. And after 30 seconds the referee stands them up. Now this guy gets out of a dominant position, one where he can't take too much damage, he stands, he gets kicked in the head and goes down. Why was the other guy able to deliver that kick? Because we have a referee who doesn't understand what he's doing, what he's looking at, and allows him to be pulled out of a dominant position. "

McCarthy says there are also little rule nuances that fans may not be aware of, from promotion to promotion or country to country, and that those rule changes get confusing for the fighters, the judges, the referees, and the fans.

"I would love to see, I don't care where you go, every fight takes place under the same rules. Sometimes there are little variations in the rules and the fans don't know it, and they think the referee is doing something wrong or the fighter should do something different and they can't."

McCarthy says that the pressure on referees is not only to get the calls right, but also to keep the fighters safe from serious injury, and that criticism from fans and promoters, especially UFC president Dana White, is unfair. Referee Steve Mazzagatti is one referee who has come under fire by the UFC president, who once said, "Steve Mazzagatti shouldn't be allowed to watch a UFC fight, never mind ref one."

"You know, I look at it both ways," says McCarthy. "Steve is not as bad as Dana makes him out to be, but you know what, you need to put Dana in Steve's position. Dana is on the outside, and everyone listens to him because he's the guy, he's the face of MMA. That's it. It's the only way it is. And you know Steve is not out there defending himself. He's a gentleman about it. It's tough. It's hard when you're Steve and you've got Dana White coming after you. It's hard not to sit there and say something back, you know? I give Steve props for being the gentleman he is even though sometimes you think, 'Dude, I think I would say something by now.' But, you know, that's a personal choice.

"Dana needs to understand what it's like to be that guy. All that weight—everyone thinks it's easy to referee. 'I could do that.' Because as you sit on a couch, or you sit as Dana sits, right in front of the Octagon—he's got his monitor that's sitting there in front of him, and Dana can see things that the referee can't. The referee needs to be able to move around and do things to create an angle so he sees what he needs to do. When you have the UFC and you have all these cameras, you've got a director who's sitting there and he's calling, 'Camera two. Go to four. Go to eight. Go back to two.' That's creating the best angle for you [the viewer] to see it. Well, the referee has got to create that angle for himself.

"I have a lot of people come to the classes that I teach. You put them in the cage with fighters and they have to move and be in the right position, and all of the sudden they're like, 'Oh my god! That is not anything like I thought it was going to be.' There is a lot to consider. And this is in a gym when there's really no pressure."

Big John teaches referee seminars and gives certifications under his COMMAND banner, which stands for Certification of Officials for Mixed Martial Arts National Development. Herb Dean also awards MMA certifications under his banner, MMARS, which is an acronym for Mixed Martial Arts Referee School.

Both Herb and John are considered the best referees in the business, though neither school is actually backed by any particular state athletic commission. They do however, follow the Unified Rules of MMA, which were developed by McCarthy, original UFC color commentator Jeff Blatnick, and matchmaker Joe Silva, in conjunction with Larry Hazzard, the New Jersey State Athletic Commissioner, and Marc Ratner, who at the time was the Executive Director of the Nevada State Athletic Commission and today is the Vice President of Regulatory Affairs for the UFC.

New Jersey was the first state to sanction MMA under the new rules in 2001, opening the doors to other states' sanctioning bodies.

Learning the rules should be priority one for proper judging of the sport, and McCarthy goes so far as to say the states should require an official process to get a license to referee and judge in MMA.

"There should be some certification," he says. "There has to be something or someone they have to go through to show their qualifications. To allow them to be in the middle, between two human beings who could possibly do something that could cause them serious injury, they have to know what they are looking at. They have to be able to prove it. There are too many people that are able to get in because they have this friend or that friend, or because they've lied about their qualifications and things like that. That's just wrong. It shouldn't happen, and it's wrong for the fighters, the fans, and the promoters. People sit there while two fighters go at it, and if the referee screws up, the fans blame the promoter, who has no say in who the commission gives him as a referee. And so, it [certification] helps the commission, it helps the promoter, it helps the fighters and the fans. It helps everyone if you have somebody in there that knows what they are doing.

> ❝The thing with fighting and with people," he continues, "and this is what I tell all referees: a fan buys their ticket, and they pay their hard-earned money to go watch and to be entertained. They have certain expectations. But, what they don't have is the responsibility that's associated with it. So, if they go to the show, and one of the fighters in the show gets seriously hurt because the referee doesn't stop the fight when maybe they should—the guy takes too many blows and is unable to recover from what has occurred and unable to come back and be normal, is permanently altered in his life, or his life is taken by that decision not to do something—the fan who's on the outside? They can (John puts his hands up in the air), 'I didn't do it.'❞

"They can walk away and say, 'Oh I saw it. He should have stopped it.' But they don't have any responsibility associated with it. The referee, when he's in there, he is responsible for the safety of those fighters. And you know a long time ago I came up with, and it was at UFC 3 that I said, *'I need to be able to stop the fight if the fighter cannot intelligently defend themselves. I've got to be able to stop the fight.'*

"And it might be that they can't intelligently defend themselves just for a second. Their eyes go back, their brain housing group is not functioning the normal way. Is it the next shot, if I let it go through, is that going to be the one that's going to permanently injure this person? It may not, but it may. And I want to be able to get in there and stop it so at least I know I did the right thing. The referee has got to live with whatever they do. If they don't get in and someone does get permanently injured, they have to live with it for the rest of their life. They have to look in the mirror and ask, 'Did I do the right thing?' Every time they look in the mirror they're going to know. Whether they tell you or not, they're going to know, 'I didn't do my job. I didn't stop it when I should have.' They have got to live with that for the rest of their lives. It's not a good thing to go home with."

The questions most fans really want to ask Big John, though, is what happened between him and the UFC.

The answer is pretty simple. John says he was caught between being a UFC employee and a referee for hire for state athletic commissions, and since he discovered that he couldn't please everyone, he decided it would be best to just please himself.

He took a hiatus from refereeing to be a commentator for The Fight Network in Canada. While there, John didn't sugar-coat his thoughts about the state of refereeing in MMA, as he's done here in this interview, and some of the things he said ruffled more than a few feathers, with both promoters and athletic commissioners. Couple that with Big John accepting a color commentating position with the short-lived Affliction fight promotion, which challenged the UFC, and it's pretty easy to see why there was no turning back—at least right away—for either side.

It's been a few years since the height of the unofficial rift between Big John McCarthy and those bodies, and little by little Big John has been hired again to ref UFC events, putting him back inside the Octagon that made him so famous in the first place.

"I made the decision [to leave] based off, I felt I was stuck. I was doing things with the UFC and they were paying for some things for me, and then the commission would ask me to do things and the UFC didn't want me to do it and that became a problem. I couldn't make the two entities happy. So I figured it was time for me to walk away because, 'I can't do this.' I love the UFC. I started with the UFC. I've been to court several times for the UFC. I was there when everyone was saying how bad it is, and I was trying to get people to understand. I love what the UFC is, I love what the UFC has become. It is the No. 1 show out there and they do a phenomenal job. I hear people say, 'John doesn't like the UFC.' That's ridiculous. I have not missed one UFC ever. How does that say that I hate it? After doing the Roger

Huerta/Clay Guida fight [his final fight], I woke up the next day and I thought, 'Oh my God, what did I do?' And I wasn't planning on being a commentator. I was offered to do something and I looked at it as my way of staying in the sport, and, 'Well, I'm not going to be pissing people off.'

"That didn't work out too well," he says, bursting out laughing.

CHAPTER 6

JOSH THOMSON, STRIKEFORCE FIGHTER

Former Strikeforce lightweight champ Josh Thomson and I meet up at American Kickboxing Academy in San Jose, home to fighters Cain Velasquez, Jon Fitch, Mike Swick, Dan Cormier, Cung Le, and Josh Koscheck.

Thomson got his nickname, the Punk, here at this very gym. Being the smallest guy at AKA takes a certain kind of attitude to survive, and what Josh lacked in size and strength, he made up for in guile and nerve.

"I give Cain the biggest headache," he says. "I'm constantly on him. He's so quiet, and I'm just like a little Chihuahua yapping at him, 'Get up, go harder, go faster! Do this! Do that!' So that's kind of how it all came about. I used to do little sneaky things to get out of submissions, too. Instead of tapping I would do the fish hook or whatever. Just things you couldn't do in a real fight."

These days, Josh has outgrown the nickname, but once a fighter has brand recognition it's hard to shed the past.

"I've had it since I first came out to AKA. So it's been hard to shake. And it's not gone, let me just tell you. I'll always have it in the gym. It won't ever go anywhere. We're keeping it."

Thomson's been fighting since 1997, and he's been with Javier Mendez at AKA for more than a decade. He's fought in Japan, Hawaii, the UFC, Strikeforce, and many other promotions in many other countries. Perhaps his biggest rival in the business today is Gilbert Melendez, the No. 2 ranked lightweight in the world and the man who beat Thomson and took his Strikeforce belt.

"He's got a lot of power in his right hand," says Thomson of Melendez, a man he respects as a person and a fighter. "The one thing you can never question about him is his heart and determination. That guy will push. He'll push through anything. You rock him, he'll come forward. Most fighters may step back. You know, you hit him and you rock him, he wants to come forward. He wants to hit you back. That's the fighter in us."

"I started fighting in small shows," Thomson says about his journey through MMA. "I would have to say my first fight was back in '97. So then from then on, it's been a joy. I just keep fighting. We started fighting like in fairgrounds, casinos, things like that. And I had a couple, probably about five or six fights in Idaho and then I moved down here and started training with Bob Cook and Javier Mendez [manager and owner/head trainer of AKA], and the rest is history."

1997 was the pre-Zuffa UFC era, when mixed martial arts was banned from cable and pay-per-view. It had been relegated to Native American reservation casinos or flyover states that sanctioned the sport before the bigger market cities jumped on board. He's seen the evolution of the sport firsthand.

"I thought the way the sport was going at the time, it was growing so fast, I didn't know where it was going to go. I don't think anybody did. I saw a different end [of the fight business]. I saw the struggles from the UFC, Strikeforce, Dream, Pride. I saw the struggles and… for us, we hear all the stuff that goes on behind the scenes. But, the fans and just normal people, politicians, they don't understand that. So they think that everything is just peachy. They think the sport is growing and everything, but we saw—I saw it from the very beginning, when the UFC wasn't making any money, how they lost their ass and Strikeforce too, building itself as a promotion.

"With all the things that the UFC has done and Strikeforce has done, and Pride, and now Dream, all of these organizations, they're the best in the world and they've done so well in making sure that they've built a sport, a legitimate sport. And people can watch. The average fan can watch. With a little bit of knowledge they can understand what is going on, on the ground, on the feet. Now it's not just two fat guys laying on each other or just trying to knock each other out."

Today it's easy to forget that not so many years ago, fighters actually paid promoters just for the opportunity to fight. The younger guys who sign big contracts today are fortunate that guys like Josh Thomson came before them and helped build the sport into the juggernaut it is today.

> ❝ My first fight I had to pay $25 to fight. My second fight I made $150, and I'd been called on three days' notice to fight. The third fight was $300, and I got called on a week's notice. Those were the times we were dealing with back then. I mean, I might as well have just been at the bar starting a fight with someone, that's how close it was. 'Hey, will you come and fight? We'll pay you this.' It was an experience. But I wouldn't give it back for anything. I mean, I enjoyed every moment of it all, and it's been great. It's led me to where I am today. ❞

Josh explains the process fighters go through, from getting licensed and tested to picking a training camp.

"Each state is different in what they recommend, so you have to do medicals. That's blood work: Hepatitis A, B, C, and HIV. You have to do neurological exams, MRIs, everything to make sure the fighter is safe [to fight]. That goes for every state. So if most of my fights are in California and I go fight in Nevada, then I have to do all the same stuff over there. I have to get re-licensed over there. My California license doesn't transfer. So I'm redoing all the medical work again."

All of this is at the fighter's expense, by the way. While one would think that a promoter would take care of all of that kind of stuff, that's simply not the way things are done. Josh says that's just part of the process.

"It makes you appreciate what you're doing. When you see all the results come in, it [makes you appreciate] your safety. It makes you really understand that, 'Hey, I'm paying for my safety.' That's really what it is. As far as the licensing, we pay for that as well. I paid for my corners and their licenses. I'm sure some people have their corners pay for themselves, but I feel like they're doing me a favor being in my corner. I've worked with them, and they've been with me my whole career basically. Bob Cook has been with me since my fourth or fifth fight. So, you know, I don't plan on not paying for him to be there for me."

At 155 pounds, Thomson fights in what has become the deepest division in all of mixed martial arts, particularly since the UFC has merged the WEC into its stable of fighters. Penn, Edgar, Alvarez, Melendez, Gomi, Sotiropoulos, Pellegrino, Aoki, Miller, Florian, Kawajiri, Sakarai, and on and on. A list of dangerous fighters at lightweight could go on for at least two pages. With so many top-level guys in one division, Thomson says it gets hard to determine who really is No. 1, until they fight each other.

"You have three to four different organizations. You have top guys in all those organizations. It just helps build the What Ifs. 'What if I would have fought this guy from here and that guy from there?' And until we all fight each other, you'll never know. That's why it's such an [interesting] division but…the chances of us all being in one organization are becoming slimmer."

I don't know if it's something in the water, but most of the lightweight fighters in the U.S. are based on the East Coast. UFC champ Frankie Edgar has the advantage of training with Dream fighter and Bellator champ Eddie Alvarez, as well as fellow UFC lightweight Jim Miller. Kenny Florian trains with Kurt Pellegrino, etc.

For Josh, the best lightweight in a 25-mile radius is Melendez, and obviously he can't train with a guy he's bound to fight again, so I ask him if it's difficult to find training partners to spar with.

"I'm considered one of the bigger '55-pounders," he says, "So, to be honest, I train a lot with Koscheck, Fitch, and Swick. Those guys are at the top at the welterweight division. If I can train with them, then I don't have a problem with '55-pounders. One thing that goes through my mind is that I know if I can get one takedown in three rounds against Koscheck, I'm going to be able to take a '55-pounder down. But it's funny that you say that. In the last couple years we've developed our '55-pound weight class, but for the longest time I've been the only one here. Now I have Justin Wilcox. I've got Brian Travers and J.J. Ambrose, so these guys are all now fighting at 155. They're here in my gym and they're helping me train every day."

One thing that sets AKA apart from some of the other professional MMA gyms is that people come here directly out of college. Guys like Josh Koscheck and Cain Velasquez were built from the ground up, whereas Greg Jackson, for instance, tends to pick up fighters who are already established but are looking for better direction in their careers.

"It happens with Crazy Bob, DeWayne Zinkin, and Javier. That's how it happens," says Josh. "There's not one of our fighters who came to us with a whole lot of [experience]. Greg Jackson's people tend to already have a career. Most of them were already in the UFC. Then they went there. I was here with four or five fights, and like I said, making $300 a fight. Cain's straight out of college. Fitch is basically straight out of college. Nate Moore, straight out of college. We have tons of guys. Koscheck came off the wrestling circuit. He just walked off the mat. Threw his headgear on the mat and walked off the mat and said, 'I'll be there on Monday.' He showed up on Monday and started training. That was how Koscheck ended up with us. He's like, 'I'm done with wrestling. I'm ready to fight.' I was there that day at the U.S. Open [wrestling tournament]."

Josh says Javier Mendez could charge admission to sparring day at AKA.

"It's packed with people, and the great thing is we allow our students to come in and train. The ones that have the ability to come in and train with us, we allow them to come in and work with us a little bit. We can always learn a little something from them, too. You have the guys that come in and they're afraid of us and they run, so it's learning how to cut the ring off. You gotta be patient. You gotta pick 'em apart. And you know, there are guys that have good jiu-jitsu, so you're stopping their takedown. These are the students. We have a lot of good students. Dave Camarillo has built up a great jiu-jitsu program here. There are 60-70 good jiu-jitsu kids that are in here and they come and do our training and they help us out on the ground."

Any fighter will tell you, however, that he could be sparring the best in the world and never get hurt, but two minutes of sparring with a beginner is bound to result in an injury of some sort.

"They don't have the self-control. They spazz out. They're thinking they're going to impress us by doing a flip over our guard or something, and the next thing you know we butt heads and you have a cut and you're thinking, 'Oh, I shouldn't have grappled with this idiot.' That's generally what happens. They're real stiff. They don't know how to flow. The whole Bruce Lee, 'Flow like water,' they don't have that. Also, we'll grapple, but in a five-minute round they're tired after two minutes because they're just trying so hard to impress us, I think."

Thomson has been hampered with injuries throughout his career, some that have prevented him from fighting for a year or more. Being in the fight business, one is bound to get injured, either in training or during a bout, but I wondered why Josh was prone to get hurt more than some others.

"You know what the biggest problem is with me? I'm someone who does too much. But I can't change, because I'm also that person that feels like if I don't do that, then I'm not ready. I'm that kid who'll get up in the morning and run two or three miles and then I'll train at noon. I'll do sparring, and spar hard for an hour and a half, and then grapple five hard rounds and do some bag work. That's like two hours, and then I'll go home for an hour and sleep and eat and then I'll go train with my strength and conditioning coach at four o'clock. I'll do that for an hour, come back home, eat, rest for an hour, then I'll go do hard cardio. I've already run in the morning, but I still have to do my sprint cardio at night. Sometimes I'll do three to four sessions a day. Your body just gets torn down, but if I don't do it, then I don't feel ready to go. And if I don't feel mentally ready, I go into the fight with jitters and nerves.

"I don't ever get nervous. That's why. I don't get nervous because I know I've done everything I possibly can to be the best. Just put every possible effort into this, and if I get hurt, I get hurt. But at least I know that I'm doing it, doing something. I'm training my ass off and making sure that I can lay it all out there on the line. If you saw my second fight with Gilbert Melendez, I left it all out there. Whether I lost, whether I won, whatever the deal was, it was because I laid it all out there."

During this interview we started dropping names of different Strikeforce fighters he could face inside the cage. We talk about Jorge Gurgel, K.J. Noons, and J.Z. Cavalcante a little. Then I bring up the TMZ cell phone video of Roger Huerta knocking out a guy in front of a Texas club after witnessing the dude punch a woman square in the face, dropping her to the street like a sack of potatoes.

Even Dana White tweeted that Huerta did the right thing.

"I gotta say, I'm with the public on this. I support him 100 percent—and I never thought that Dana White and I would agree on something—but that guy deserved it. You know, anybody who hits a girl like that…he definitely got what he deserved."

Many have said that what Roger Huerta did that night was act like a martial artist. He used his training and his skill to stick up for a woman who was attacked by a man three times her size. If you watch that video, Huerta himself was much smaller than the guy. But Huerta pounds the shit out of him. I ask Thomson what he thinks it means to be a martial artist in MMA.

"I didn't come up doing martial arts so it's hard for me to say. Some of these fighters now, they talk about being a martial artist and I don't think they understand what the concept of being a martial artist is. It bugs me. I hate to say it, but I'm just a fighter. I really am. It's different because I was raised this way. My dad used to make me stick up for my brothers. He made me go out on the front lawn and fight one time because someone was picking on my brother. He just watched. I mean, those were the things that I grew up with. Everyone always says, 'Are you mad at your father for that?' or, 'Don't you look back and regret that?' I say no, I don't. Not at all, because look at my job now. So all it did was just point me in the right direction. Life is full of choices. I made the choice to do what I'm doing and I wouldn't change that for the world. I don't resent my father for it.

> **"**But, no, I don't consider myself a martial artist. I consider myself a professional athlete—one of the best in the world—and a fighter. I love fighting. This is what I do. I started off wrestling, and I went from there to learning how to do some kickboxing and then a little bit of jiu-jitsu, and then I just started fighting. And as I became addicted to the sport, I realized that it has the same effect on you as martial arts because you're putting so much time and energy into it. You learn how to control your emotions. You [can't just be out there fighting] in the streets. There is a lot of discipline that goes into this, and it's taught me a lot. And so, yeah, in that aspect, it is like a martial art. For me it's different.**"**

Back in 2000, Thomson was on a lake cruise in Idaho with a group of friends when an alcohol-fueled argument with another group turned into a full-on brawl. Thomson choked a man out, almost killing him. He was charged with felony aggravated assault and sentenced to three years, but was released after six months for good behavior.

Like most fighters, Josh Thomson felt the pressure from his family and friends to quit fighting and take a more traditional path in life. At least nowadays it's easy to say, 'Watch Spike or Versus or HDNet or *SportsCenter* or get the pay-per-view this weekend. That's what I do.'

But back in 1997 when Thomson started fighting, it wasn't so easy to explain to people what MMA was.

"My worst critics were my family," he says. "'What are you doing with your life? You were in college. What happened?' And I was like, 'Well I'm tired of being in college. I'm tired of wrestling.' But I wanted to be in a competitive sport. That fire in you is not gone. It doesn't go away. I still have that burn. I can't get rid of it. So, until that goes away, I don't think I want to stop. But then there's that thin line of understanding when you don't have it anymore. I know that. For a lightweight, we lose it a little bit faster [than heavier weights] because the first thing that goes for a lightweight is their speed. And you have to be able to keep up with the new lightweights who still have that speed. With heavier guys, they can get away with it, because most of them just lay on each other, let's be honest. You know. They're not the most exciting. If they can't knock you out, they just lay on you."

I'm glad Josh brought this up, because I've heard the heavier-weight fighters remark that they get tired of hearing that lightweight fighters are more exciting. They say the only reason that's so is because the lighter-weight guys don't have knockout power. So when they get in one of those slugfests that fans love so much, they're able to trade and look good doing it, because neither of them ever goes down. Josh disagrees.

"No, lightweights are more exciting because we keep the fight at a constant pace and it goes up and down, up and down, fast, fast, fast. We're constantly picking up the pace. I mean, my fight with Gilbert—both of them, actually—we never stopped. When you hit the second round with a heavyweight, they're pretty much done. I mean, they're laying on each other. They're…unless your name is Cain Velasquez and you're going to keep moving and keep moving and keep moving, odds are they're going to be laying on you."

Cain Velasquez is said to be able to go at a crazy pace during training, and since the Punk trains with him, I ask him his impression of the UFC heavyweight champ.

"If I could move like that, it'd be…and I'm a lightweight. I can't move like him. I can't. He wrestles at angles. He's constantly striking.

He's constantly moving. He doesn't stop and he won't stop until he wins the scramble. One thing I think a lot of the fighters here in AKA have picked up from him is that the wrestling doesn't stop once you get taken down. That's when it starts. It's like, that's when the wrestling starts and that's—it's the same with striking. I've landed my shot, okay, and it doesn't go away. I gotta move and get out and then land again. Or get the takedown, whatever it is. That's the one thing we've learned from each other. Cain is just a genetic freak, and he's shaped his fighting style off the way he used to wrestle. It's go, go, go, go. No one's going to take that away from him. That's his style." Anyone who saw the way Cain thoroughly demolished ex-champ Brock Lesnar knows exactly what Josh is talking about.

One thing Thomson does share with Velasquez is a Mexican heritage. His mother is Mexican and his late father was Caucasian. He says the death of his father is what pushed him over the top in the MMA world.

"It pushed me harder; it really did. I won my title right after that. See, I was raised by my dad and then my two grandmothers. They pretty much raised me. So, I lost my dad and then, less than 10 months later, I lost one of my grandmothers. So it was rough. It was a rough ride. My family has always been there for me. No matter how much of a pain in the ass they are—and the majority of them are—they're always there. I consider myself one of the most loyal people there is, especially with my family. I always put them first, no matter what."

In the past, Thomson has said that one of his goals was to fight in the UFC. Check. Another was to win a world championship. Check. So, if he retired tomorrow, would he be satisfied?

"One hundred percent, I'd be done," he says. "Had I made a little bit more money, you know, in the past, I would be done. I would love to wash my hands right now and walk away from this sport, to be honest. I want to start doing other things. I would love to commentate. I would love to be a ref. I would love to be a cut guy, doesn't matter. I know how to wrap hands. I know how to do cuts. You know, I feel like I speak well enough to be a commentator, it depends. There are a lot of things I would love to do, but I want to be—I'd love to be part of this sport."

Thomson also sheds some insight on the most powerful man in MMA, Dana White.

"The Dana White that you guys know today is not the Dana White I knew back then. The Dana White I knew back then was somebody that, when he met me in Hawaii when I fought Kid Yamamoto, before I got home there were three boxes of clothes and shirts and hats, just letting you know the appreciation he had for you. He signed me right on the spot. I met him in Hawaii right after a fight and he was like, 'Hey, welcome to the UFC.' I didn't even win the fight. It was a no contest, but he was so excited and he was happy about it. I don't know if he still has that relationship with his fighters anymore, but I look at Dana as, he brought me to where I am. I appreciate him for that and I appreciate the Fertittas a lot. The UFC, that was my goal in life. And I respect them 100 percent for that. But the Dana White now…he's dealing with a whole different perspective of the sport. There's so much more involved, with all the TV stuff. He's a busy, busy man, you know?

"But now, I think the difference is that Scott Coker is someone who is building his organization. He understands the fighters and where they're coming from, like Dana used to. Not just in a business sense, either. With Scott it's different. He has the business idea of it all, from K1 to Strikeforce. He has all the connections with TV. But I can still call up Scott Coker and say, 'Hey, you want to have dinner?' 'Yeah, sure let's meet, let's talk.' And we'll meet anywhere we want. You know, with Dana, I think that time has lapsed. Schedule an appointment.

"The other thing is that the UFC has saturated the market. In a sport so young, there's just not enough talent to have as many fights as they're putting on. That's what the difference is between the UFC and Strikeforce. We have A-level fighters in Strikeforce, and so A-level fighters are always fighting A-level guys, because that's all we have. He signed all the A-level guys and he's having us fight each other. In the UFC they've saturated the market so much that now there's just fights to fight. You know, there's no purpose. They're not going anywhere. It's like a boxing card, with the two main events and then nothing. You have the two main attractions, and the rest of the card is just fights they threw together. Guys you probably haven't even heard of."

I don't necessarily agree with Josh, and I tell him that any MMA event, including Strikeforce, doesn't resemble boxing at all. The undercards are always interesting and exciting, even if we've never heard of those fighters before.

"No, I agree with that," Josh says. "That used to be the fact, too. That used to be the case with the UFC. That's slowly starting, like I said, it is slowly starting to fade away. And it's not because they don't want to put on good fights. Joe Silva does a great job. But the thing is, they're putting on so many fights, they don't have enough good, A-level talent to do that. I mean, let's be honest, some of the beginning fights, they're not great fights. In Strikeforce they have four [on a card], and I think they're going to talk about adding a fifth fight every time. These are all A-level guys that are always going to be fighting each other. Next time you see us fight, it'll be Robbie Lawler and Cung and Frank and somebody else. There will be me and Gilbert, and it'll be Gilbert and Aoki and me and JZ. Those are the fights that people want to see, and we have a whole card of that. The UFC now, there's four fights a month. It's not their fault. It's not. There's just not enough talent in the sport."

Like most fighters, Josh views fighting as a job. He holds no ill will toward his opponents, including his biggest rival, Gil Melendez.

"We're very good friends," he says. "I actually just went to his baby shower a couple weeks back and yeah, we're really good friends. We swap a lot of information, as far as [professional expectations]. You know, just helping each other like, 'Hey, Strikeforce wants to re-sign me and I want to re-sign with them. Are you going to stay?' To be honest, I look up to him. You know, I think he's looked up to me, too. We've talked about it and it's been, 'I've beaten you, you've beaten me, and we're cool with calling it even. But if we want to make good money, let's fight again.' We know that. And so now we want to attack this in the right way. Just both of us keep winning and we'll fight each other again and let's make some money. Like you said, Mike, we want to make sure that it's focused toward having a life for our family, our kids and making sure they have what they need."

All of that said, Thomson trains at AKA, where guys such as Josh Koscheck and Jon Fitch and Mike Swick say they'll never fight against one another, even if Josh and Jon are the No. 2 and 3 fighters in their division. Why is it okay for Josh to fight a close friend like Gil and not okay for those guys?

"Well, Gilbert and I are friends. We're not teammates," he explains. "Gilbert used to come in and train with us all the time. Three days a week, he and Jake Shields—but now that Jake is with the UFC and, you know, Gilbert is fighting in Strikeforce, they don't come to the gym anymore and train. But regardless, I'm not going to shun him if I see him on the street. I just saw him last Sunday, him and his wife. She's due soon and I just like to check up and say, 'Hey, how you doing? How's the baby, and how you feeling?' But, as far as the organization stuff, all that stuff is left at the door. I train with Kos and Fitch and Swick and Cain and those guys. When they walk through the door, there's not a big stamp on their forehead that says UFC. They're my teammates and we're all fighters. So, that's what we look at."

Josh tiptoes around the question so I push him a little harder on the issue of teammates fighting each other. If I'm a promoter like Dana White, I have every right to ask two guys who are at the top of one of my divisions to fight each other, because it's good business, plain and simple.

"You want to see them fight? I can watch them fight every day. Monday, Wednesday, Friday, Saturday. It doesn't matter. They're here sparring their asses off, and to be honest, they're going to lay it on the line here, so there's no reason for them to go out there and do it. I think Fitch is doing the right thing right now. He is approaching it the way he should. There is no reason to even talk about that. We used to have this old saying, 'Hey, if it's going to be for the title, you might as well.' But with Fitch, guys are different. They train with him all the time. And why would I try and take a title away from my friend? If you start thinking about it that way, Fitch has the body frame to go up to 185. He walks around at 200 pounds. So he's like, you know, 'I'll put on a little more weight and I'll got to '85.' He doesn't mind. He doesn't care. If he wants to give it a try, give it a try. If it doesn't work, he can always come back to 170."

We talk about Russian heavyweight, and one of Strikeforce's most marketable fighters, Fedor Emelianenko, who lost for the first time in his career in 2010 against Fabricio Werdum after getting caught in a triangle choke. Fedor is a guy who's made more money than he can spend in his hometown of Stary Oskol in Northern Russia. I ask if the MMA community expects too much from him, when he seemingly doesn't care about rankings or making money.

"No, I just think that since he didn't sign with the UFC, people want to criticize everything he does now," Josh says. "And what they have to understand is that, like you said, when money is not an issue, then what's the point? I'm doing it because I love the sport. That goes a long way for a lot of people when you live in areas like that. Money is not a concern, so then what do I have to worry about? You know, I do it because I love the sport. I think in his eyes he thought it was a better way for him to help build the sport versus just being a doll for a promotion to use. Who knows?"

Another fighter who tends to make headlines outside of fighting, or because of his antics while fighting, is Anderson Silva. MMA fans know what happened first in Montreal against Thales Leites, and then in Abu Dhabi against Damian Maia, when he danced around the ring, hardly fighting at all, and in main events.

> **"**He's been hanging out with Floyd Mayweather too much. That's my personal opinion. It's a joke. I think the worst part about it is that he can fight. The guy can fight. He has proved that he can fight. But, I think now he's just become so in tune with doing what he wants because he can get away with it that it's become a joke now. His first fights, he didn't do any of that. He went out there, got the job done, got 'em in, got 'em out. That was it. Now, it's kind of like a joke.**"**

"You're talking about making Jon Fitch fight Koscheck, make him [Silva] fight at 205. And I'm not talking about James Irving. I'm talking about Shogun, I'm talking about Rampage. Make him fight somebody and see what happens from there. The thing with that organization is that they run the show, they do what they want—they've done a great job—but you can't put pressure on one fighter to fight his teammate and then you see another fighter not performing at all, getting booed out of the ring. How can you not put pressure on that?"

CHAPTER 7

BAS RUTTEN, MMA PIONEER

Bas "El Guapo" Rutten was born on February 24, 1965, in Holland. He was a UFC heavyweight champion, King of Pancrase, a kickboxer, and an overall badass who fought some of the most legendary battles in the history of MMA with the likes of Frank Shamrock, Kevin Randleman, Guy Mezger, Maurice Smith, Masakatsu Funaki, and Minoru Suzuki.

He also perfected the liver punch, a debilitating knockout blow that used to be known solely as the left hook to the body.

> "I should have trademarked *liver punch*," says Bas. "I started that, and whenever I hear someone say *liver punch* I think, 'That's cool, I started that.' But the first time I fought Muay Thai I was a tough guy, and my hands were up here and then bam, I get hit with the liver punch. And I'm going down and I feel it. It hurts very bad. It's better to get knocked out with a kick to the head because you wake up in the dressing room and say, 'What happened?' But with the liver punch, man, you are aware of the pain and I don't know what's going on inside the body, but I know it hurts."

Bas is one of the most charismatic characters in MMA, and these days he is the co-host of *Inside MMA* on HDNet, where he serves as foil and analyst to straight man Kenny Rice. His YouTube commercials for apparel company Tokyo Five have gone viral, and it's plain to see that Rutten has the acting chops to take his career to the next level. He could easily find himself one day starring in a buddy comedy with Jackie Chan about two aging kickass fighters out for one more adventure.

I've gotten to know Bas because our shows are on the same network, and we've been to fan expos, awards shows, and of course, fights, together. But the most fun I have with Bas is at dinner after said events, where the ties are loosened and everyone is relaxed. Bas is, simply put, one of the most generous people I know.

Last year I taped an episode of TLC's *Orange County Chopper* with the guys from Head Rush Apparel Company and UFC light heavyweight Phil Davis. The series patriarch, Paul Teutul, Sr., began talking to us about mixed martial arts. However, he didn't talk about the latest UFC championship bout, nor did he talk about the cultural phenomenon the sport has become. He talked about the hilarious *Bas Rutten's Lethal Street Fighting* videos on YouTube. I was blown away.

Besides being one of MMA's pioneers, fans revere him for his sense of humor. "I think I get it from my dad's side. We got the Rutten humor," says Bas. "My wife always says, 'You know, nobody likes your humor. They only laugh because they are afraid of you, because you are psycho; that's what you are.' So I got this really selective group of friends, and everybody likes that kind of humor, but yeah sometimes, when I am doing *Inside MMA*, you see me writing things down. This is like, really crazy stuff that I want to say, and if I don't write it down, I say it. I really have to tone back, tone back, tone back. I am learning to deal with it though, because I'm doing more work, but I got these funny ideas. I think it's funny, but a lot of people think its offensive."

Believe it or not, it wasn't always so funny for Rutten. When he was in grade school he suffered from a devastating bout of eczema, a skin disease that forced Bas to scratch himself bloody, bringing out the bullies in the process.

"I had this horrible skin disease everywhere, and I had to wear gloves," says Rutten. "So I was the leper in school. At the time Michael Jackson wasn't there yet, so it wasn't cool to put white gloves on, especially not if you see this colored stuff coming through, so I was bullied a lot.

"There would be days that if I would [just scratch], it would burst, and pus and blood would come out. My family would send sheets, blankets, old blankets that my mother would rip in pieces and mummify me every night. And at night I would scratch it off again and the next night they would do it again."

The experience left Bas feeling insecure and unable to fit in with his peers, and he says it was Bruce Lee who showed him the light.

> ❝We were on vacation in Paris and my brother and I saw *Enter The Dragon* and that was it. From that moment on all I wanted to do was martial arts," he says, adding that Bruce Lee was the first real mixed martial artist.
>
> "He was already experimenting with different things. We saw him making takedowns, we saw him doing an armbar in *Enter The Dragon* in the opening scene against Samo Hung—although when I see the armbar now I go, like, 'Not a real good armbar.' But he was experimenting with it, so I'm pretty sure that if he would have grown up in this age, he would have for sure done MMA. He was always evolving his style. He never liked it that people would just say, 'Okay, this is it.' It needs to be evolving.❞

However, no matter how enthusiastic the young Rutten was after watching Bruce Lee do his thing in the movies, convincing his conservative mother and father to allow him to take martial arts classes was a chore in itself.

"They wouldn't let me take class, but finally my next-door neighbor was a girl and her boyfriend was the cool guy in the neighborhood, and he took class so they finally let me do it."

Bas did well in class, and even as a white belt his confidence rose, and pretty soon he was giving it back to the bullies who used to pick on him in school. But that's exactly what his parents were afraid of, and karate was out after one street fight.

"I took on the biggest bully in the neighborhood and one punch, knocked him out, broke his nose and that was it for class until I moved out of the house, around 20 years old, and once I was on my own I put everything into martial arts," he says.

Bas began kickboxing in Holland, but after knocking 40 guys out, he says he became disillusioned with the Dutch audience because after one loss, fans were saying he couldn't fight. He vowed to never fight in Holland again.

"I said I was not going to fight anymore in Holland because it was a dumb audience. They didn't respect the people," says Rutten. "Now, I still wanted to do something with martial arts because it always intrigued me. So we came up with doing these crazy martial arts shows to music. We break-danced, nunchucked, broke boards, and all that kind of stuff, and then that picked up and suddenly we're doing it at events."

It was during this time that Bas discovered his love for performing and began to develop the comedic chops he is revered for today.

"We put in a little comedy, and the comedy picked up real fast and people started to really react to that, so we started making it more of a comedy show, but with great martial arts in it. And we would do crazy stuff. I would come out in a costume, with a flip and a somersault backward, and that's how we would walk up to the ring."

It was at one of these shows that someone from the Japanese professional wrestling association, RINGS, suggested that Bas try "free-fighting," which is what MMA was called back then. Bas tried it and was choked out pretty quick. Frustrated with his poor performance, Rutten hit the gym hard and quickly learned the submission game, giving him a solid foundation for mixed martial arts. Already an accomplished kickboxer, the addition of a solid ground game would put Rutten on his now legendary path to MMA stardom.

> ❝One day my wife tells me, 'You're going to be a famous fighter in Japan.' And I go, 'No, because I'm not going to fight anymore.' She says, 'Yeah, you said you won't fight in Holland, but you are going to Japan'—whatever. Six months later I get a phone call to go to Amsterdam to do a tryout. [Masakatsu] Funaki [co-founder of Pancrase] is there, and they're looking for new fighters. I go to the tryout and this world champion from RINGS had to spar with me, and the TV was there so obviously he tried to hurt me. So I knocked him out. ❞

"They say, 'We want him,' and two months later I'm in Japan and that was it."

Pancrase was very popular in Japan. It's where many now legendary MMA fighters got their start. Fighters like Frank Shamrock, Ken Shamrock, Guy Mezger, Josh Barnett, and Rutten, all of whom, at one time or another, held the title of King of Pancrase (champion).

Pancrase is taken from *Pankration*, a sport in the ancient Olympic games that focused on shoot wrestling. Many MMA fans and observers of the sport—right or wrong—assume many fights in Pancrase were "worked" fights. In other words, the outcomes were predetermined. Rutten says he never saw any evidence of this, nor was he ever approached.

"I heard of that, but they never asked me to do it," he says. "One day Funaki asked me to go to dinner and I thought for sure they were going to ask me to work a fight, and we have a very nice dinner and it never came up. So I say, 'Can I say something? I thought for sure you were going to ask me,' and they said, 'No you. We would never ask you,' so that's that."

When it comes right down to it, Bas Rutten loves to fight.

"There's nothing like it," he says. "The lights. The pressure to perform. Trying out different moves, like, you try something and see how your opponent reacts, and then bam, you try it and it works. Finishing guys off is always good. Knockouts are preferable, but I love a good submission, too."

Like many fighters who fought in Japan, Bas says the audience there is far more educated and more respectful of the fight game than say, here in America.

"They are very respectful," he says. "They actually understand that the people in the ring or in the cage are the pros. They know what they are doing. Unlike everywhere else on the planet. 'Do this, do that, do this, do that.' Everybody knows better."

In fact, when he knocked out a superstar Japanese fighter he was surprised to find that he wasn't run out of the country.

"They were handing me babies to kiss," he says. "In Holland you'd need a bodyguard to get out of there, but in Japan they put me on the cover of newspapers and wanted my autograph. It was a surreal experience."

Rutten owns a 10,000-square-foot martial arts school called Elite MMA in West Lake Village outside of Los Angeles, where he trains a wide spectrum of students, from professionals to customers just looking to stay in shape. Having dedicated his life to martial arts, he's extremely critical of people, even so-called professional fighters, who call themselves martial artists.

"Traditional martial arts as a base, it's good for your kids; it's good to learn discipline. But nowadays it's just mixed martial arts. They live in a house with five other guys and they don't need another job, because they are 'professional mixed martial artists,'" he says with a sneer.

"They're not. They're cage fighters," he says. "They get these business cards that say 'Professional Fighter.' I call them the business card guys. They got a picture of themselves on the front of the card all pumped up and covered with sweat and they go to bars and hand them out to the chicks, and I go, 'Man, just focus on becoming good, becoming a real fighter.'"

Bas says in order to become a real fighter one needs to be determined.

"BJ Penn is a determined guy. He didn't need to choose this path because he was very comfortable, yet he chooses this path and does so on a phenomenal level. Those are the real guys. These business card fighters will tap out everyone in the gym, but in a fight, under the lights, they can't perform," he says. "You know, it's the guy who can do everything the same under pressure what he does in a dojo. And once you can conquer that, you can stay calm under pressure, you are good to go."

Bas believes that training to be a fighter is different than training to be any other type of athlete, because of the explosiveness of the sport.

> **❝** I train two hours a day, one in the morning and one in the afternoon. Many people say you need six hours a day, but I say we're not running marathons. We need to have energy to fight. When I warm up I'm insane. Most people pass out when they warm up with me and I say, 'We haven't even started yet.' Then I go 40 minutes all out, insane workout. No rest at all. You are training your body to throw a lot of energy in a very short amount of time. That's why the fight is never the hard part. For me, and for most fighters, they'll tell you too, that training is the hard part. The fight is the easy part. **❞**

Bas also criticizes the monetization of martial arts, particularly in America, where black belts are bought and sold under the guise of self-esteem and capitalism.

"You know it's bad what I'm saying now, and a lot of people are not going to like it, but when I came to America, there were a lot of black belts who absolutely have no business being a black belt. These kids walking around with their parents, like, 'Oh he's got the 5th degree'—he doesn't know how to kick, lady! He doesn't know how to plant his feet right! You bought him a black belt, that's what happened! It's a money-making machine here. It's $75, you're waiting in line, 30 kids on a Sunday and everybody goes through their thing and they do it like morons and then they get their belt. You buy the belt, and, 'Oh, my son is a black belt.' I know what kind of black belt that is," says Bas, growing angrier and angrier by the minute.

Another subject that gets Rutten's goat is that of street fighter turned professional MMA fighter Kevin Ferguson, AKA Kimbo Slice, who trained under Bas while preparing for a fight in the now defunct EliteXC organization.

Kimbo was a South Florida brawler whose backyard fights became famous on YouTube, generating tens of millions of views. Boxing pro-moter Gary Shaw saw a marketing opportunity in Slice and sold CBS on the concept of developing an MMA promotion around Kimbo and the then face of women's MMA, Gina Carano.

While Carano served the promotion well with competitive fights, on the first national network-televised broadcasts Slice was awarded a questionable TKO against British veteran James Thomson. He was then exposed as a fraud when little known MMA journeyman Seth Petruzelli stepped in for an injured Ken Shamrock and knocked out EliteXC's star in just 14 seconds on CBS's second go at MMA.

Bas felt like Slice was not committed to being a professional.

"Where are the people like me?" he asks. "Where are the people with 500 Post-It notes on the walls, writing down moves, writing down submission techniques? I had two lines of tape throughout the whole house that I would walk on so my stance was perfect. Why can I do this and other people can't?"

By the time I interviewed Bas, Slice had joined the ranks of the many aspiring MMA fighters who looked for a chance to get into the UFC by competing on *The Ultimate Fighter*.

Slice showed a lot of heart by doing the show, a "professional" among "amateurs," and quickly won over the audience with, if not his work ethic, then his attitude. He went on to fight twice on UFC cards. In the *TUF 10* finale, he won a unanimous decision over Houston Alexander, but then lost to Matt Mitrione at UFC 113.

I rationalized to Rutten that if someone, namely Dana White, were to pay me more money than most people make in a year to step into the Octagon for a fight, ready or not, I'm going in. While that may not be a good representation of the sport, would he blame me for taking the shot—and the money?

"Deep down inside everybody wants to be a fighter. Everybody wants to kick ass. But they don't want to do the work for it. If somebody becomes a fighter, and he comes to me six weeks before his fight, and then he fights, then does nothing for four months, and comes back six weeks before his next fight to train, then you're not committed to be a fighter. Those four months you should have been training," he says, his face and familiar bald head becoming crimson with each word.

"I'm getting emotional about this as you can see, because I taught myself. I didn't have a mixed martial arts instructor like these guys have today. I would wake up in the middle of the night and wake up my wife because I thought of a submission, and I would try it out on her. And then I'd go to the gym the next day and work on it. There is no one who pulled the submissions I pulled in fights. And I taught myself. I lived fighting 24/7. Every day I would try new things. Everyone knows how to do a figure four. But if you can invent new setups for that figure four so your opponent doesn't detect [it coming], that's how you win fights, and the only way to do that is to commit. Do it. Commit yourself. Then you'll make it."

Fans of the Rutten of today may not even know what a badass he was. In Pancrase's heyday, Rutten was feared by some of the best fighters in the world. Rutten's professional record is 28–4–1, and of those 28 wins, 12 were by knockout and 13 were by submission. Only three of Bas Rutten's fights went to a decision. It's hard to even contemplate such an accomplishment in a professional fighter's career. His fight with Masakatsu Funaki, whom Bas beat to become King of Pancrase, was at the time one of the most technical battles in the ring.

Early on in the bout, Funaki caught Rutten in a knee bar that, by all accounts, should have broken Bas' ankle, or at the very least, forced the tap. Bas toughed it out, refusing to tap. Later in the fight, after breaking Funaki's nose with several open palm strikes to the face, Bas knocked him out with a knee to the head.

Through it all Funaki didn't give up, however, and Bas would go on to credit his "heart of a lion." But in the end, heart wasn't enough to win the match. Bas got the chance to avenge his earlier loss to Funaki, which had come at a time when Rutten wasn't so skilled in submission defense.

"It was great to avenge that loss," says Bas. "To me, that was the most important fight of my career right there."

What's truly amazing about Bas is how much he loves martial arts. It changed his life by giving him the confidence to face down the bullies who tormented him when he was a kid suffering from eczema, and in a way, each time he stepped into the ring as a professional he was still fighting those bullies of his past.

Rutten is very passionate about training. He gives it 100 percent in the gym, even now that he's retired from fighting. It's one of those things he can't give up, and I get the impression he'll be fighting, in one way or another, for the rest of his life.

CHAPTER 8

CAIN VELASQUEZ, UFC FIGHTER

UFC Heavyweight champion Cain Velasquez says he's goofy when it comes to love.

He proposed to his fiancée in Sydney, Australia, after knocking out Antonio Rodrigo Nogueira at UFC 110. While strolling on the beach, he faked stubbing his toe so that he could fall to one knee to ask the mother of his infant daughter, Coral, to spend the rest of her life with him.

She said yes.

However, if the fight had gone the other way, Velasquez may very well not be engaged today.

"I think if I had lost, I wouldn't have been in that kind of celebrating mood to do that kind of stuff," says Velasquez. But Cain had even more than just proposing to the woman of his dreams riding on a victory over Big Nog. A win would seal his shot at the UFC Heavyweight Champion, Brock Lesnar.

He would go on to win that, too.

One of the most anticipated heavyweight matchups in the history of the UFC took place at UFC 121 in Anaheim, California, on October 23, 2010. Velasquez faced one of the biggest and most imposing fighters to ever step into the Octagon in WWE crossover star Lesnar, who, after just four fights in his professional MMA career, was the undisputed champion.

Brock was coming off an impressive come-from-behind victory over Shane Carwin, in which he proved he had the heart of a champion after surviving a first-round demolition at the heavy hands of the challenger. Lesnar won via an arm-triangle choke in the second round, setting up the date with the Mexican-American former Arizona State University wrestling champ, Velasquez.

Velasquez wasn't so goofy on that night.

Referee Herb Dean called a stop to the bout at 4:12 into the first round as Velasquez brutalized the champion with excellent technique and devastating punch combinations, picking his shots with precision and accuracy and even taking the big man down after stuffing Lesnar's own takedown attempts with relative ease.

Standing inside the Honda Center, the atmosphere was electric, as it is whenever two big guys stand at the middle of a cage and go toe-to-toe. But there was something special in the air that night, as much was made of Velasquez's Mexican heritage. The place was buzzing with Mexican-Americans cheering on their first heavyweight hero. Brown Pride was in the air.

———

It's hot and muggy at American Kickboxing Academy in San Jose, California, where Velasquez trains under the watchful eye of Javier Mendez and alongside fellow UFC fighters such as Josh Koscheck, Mike Swick, and Jon Fitch, as well as Strikeforce standouts Cung Le and Josh Thomson.

Velasquez is boxing with a local heavyweight boxer whom he's never sparred with before.

"I told him to take it easy on him, just shadow a bit," says Mendez. "I told him no head contact."

The boxer, however, didn't get the memo, and his own trainer is ringside, yelling instructions at his charge. The kid lands a left hook to the side of Cain's head. Cain shoots a look to his corner, and Javier nods, giving Cain the green light to go a little harder.

The next time the boxer throws a combo, Velasquez sidesteps and lands a left hook to the body, dropping the kid at will. It would be about a minute and a half before he recovers. That's the type of fighter Velasquez is. He can turn it on or off with a nod or a shake of a head.

"Cain trains like a lightweight," says Mendez. "He's fast and he's relentless." Velasquez attributes his work ethic to his parents, who are migrant farm workers who travel from California to Yuma, Arizona, year-round, picking cotton, watermelon, and other crops and loading them into trucks.

"He was always working the fields," Velasquez says of his father, "picking lettuce, boxing lettuce, throwing the lettuce up in the trucks. That's what they did all day. And my mom did the same thing with him." The Mexican-American champion says he's on a mission to give fellow Chicanos a positive role model to look up to, hence the *Brown Pride* tattooed across his chest.

"I got the tattoo for all the hard work they [his parents] did to come over here to this country. They wanted to raise their family here, for a better life for us. My dad had to quit school when he was like in third grade to work in the fields and do all that other stuff. My mom had to quit school in the seventh grade. They've worked their whole lives. I've seen them work through my whole life and they've never—they just never complained that they had to go to work or do stuff like that. They just always went, did crappy work, but always got it done."

"Another reason is, growing up I didn't really have anybody that I could look up to in the media. I never thought that I could be in the limelight or play professional sports. So the reason I got the "Brown Pride" was to, you know, show people like me that hey, 'I'm Mexican, too. It can be done.'"

Velasquez is a soft-spoken, humble guy who takes a scientific approach to his fight career.

———

> **"**I get my coaches together, we watch film, we get a game plan going, and I work on the game plan, you know, eight weeks, 10 weeks before the fight, all the way up until the fight. I always have the game plan running in my head right before the fight, and that keeps me calm. I don't feel like a deer in the headlights when I walk out there with a huge crowd. So that really gets me ready.**"**

Part of the reason that Cain chose San Jose and American Kickboxing Academy to be his home was the fact that wrestlers such as Josh Koscheck, Jon Fitch, Daniel Cormier, and Bobby Lashley are there. These were guys he knew from the wrestling circuit who were becoming successful mixed martial artists.

"I think it really helped me when I first came in here," Cain says. "I kind of used them as, 'What do I need to do to get up to the point they are at?' You know, 'What kind of work ethic do I need to have? What kind of work on the jiu-jitsu, the wrestling, what road do I need to take to be successful in the sport?'"

UFC veteran heavyweight Paul Buentello was one of Cain's first training partners.

"He pretty much manhandled Paul," says Mendez. "It gave him a lot of confidence in himself."

Cain grew up in Yuma, Arizona, a state that made headlines in April 2010, when Governor Jan Brewer signed a law aimed at finding, prosecuting, and then deporting illegal immigrants—most of whom are Mexicans. Cain said the move embarrassed him.

"You know, it's hard. It definitely is hard. I'm just really ashamed to say that I'm from there and they're trying to pass that law. You know, I grew up having friends, families, that all the parents did the same thing. They all came over here for a better life for the family, for the kids. It's just a shame," he says, adding that the work his family and the families around him did were not the kind of jobs he ever heard any natural born citizens clamoring for.

"They've always worked in the fields. I've never seen any person other than Mexicans working the fields. And I would never think that anybody would want to do that. I've worked there a couple times in the summertime, and it's something that I didn't want to come back to. I definitely wanted to stay in school and try to play sports and further my education, [because I didn't want to go] back to that."

Cain said that at first, MMA was not something his parents understood, or wanted their youngest son to pursue.

"When I first told them that I want to do [MMA], my dad really didn't understand what it was. My mom didn't want me to do it. Nobody wanted me to do it. But now they see that I'm taking the right steps. I'm not just getting into it and fighting and not knowing anything. I'm training hard, doing all the stuff that I need to do to go out and win."

Attending high school in America exposed Velasquez and his siblings to organized sports that they would not have had if they stayed in Mexico. Cain took up football and played defensive line in high school. He was recruited to play at some colleges, but decided that wrestling would be his ticket to college. He was proven correct after becoming a two-time national wrestling champion for Arizona State University. He said it was in his junior year of college, however, that he noticed wrestling wasn't enough for him.

"I wanted to start striking," he says. "I'd always wanted to be in some kind of combat sport when I was younger. And you know, when I wrestled in college, I saw this sport [MMA] constantly growing and I just thought in my head, 'This would be a perfect transition for me to do what I want to do.'"

Cain said wrestling at such a high level in college is the perfect base for anyone hoping to transition into a professional mixed martial arts career.

"If you came out of a college program, your wrestling season starts at the end of October and goes all the way through March. That's a long season, with every week having a match or a tournament. A tournament could be 10 matches in one tournament. So you learn to wrestle when you're tired. You learn to wrestle when you're hurt and when you're injured. You learn to push your body when your body really can't go anymore. Your mind gets so strong that you can push yourself. It's also simple to transition to jiu-jitsu from wrestling, because you know what a good position is and what a bad position is. You have a lot of practice in those types of positions."

When Cain first started mixed martial arts competition, people would agree to a fight with him and then do a little research and back out of the fight before even stepping into the arena. This was before he had any type of reputation as an MMA fighter. Other fighters, however, would see that he was an NCAA champ and now trained at AKA, and would automatically drop out. Cain says it was a frustrating process, but that the guys in San Jose are used to that.

"That comes with shows that are small, you know? Even now, you know, they find out they're fighting a guy from this gym, from AKA, and they back out. Guys want to fight, but guys don't always want the hardest fights. They want easy fights while coming up."

Now that Velasquez has the belt, his next goal, aside from keeping it as long as he can, is to help his family buy a home of their own, and perhaps help them retire from life in the fields.

"I definitely want to be well established in the sport, as well as financially [successful] so I can give them something that they don't have as far as a home that they can own," he says, adding that winning is the key to hitting that endorsement jackpot and the big pay-per-view paydays.

———

> ❝It always comes down to winning. You've got to win, keep that belt, keep defending it. And then all that stuff will come. You just gotta stay hungry, you know? For me, this is my dream job. I love to work out for a living. I can't be behind a desk or anything like that. This is what I want to do. I mean, other guys have the same dream, too. They want to do this for their well-being, for their job. Guys just gotta stay hungry, get in the gym and train.❞

Like Lesnar, Velasquez has had a relatively short time as a UFC fighter. However, he's part of that next generation of well-rounded mixed martial artists, like Jon Jones, Frankie Edgar, and Georges St-Pierre. He's an anomaly in a division dominated mostly by big, one-dimensional fighters with either a wrestling (Lesnar), jiu-jitsu (Mir), or striking (Carwin) background. Cain's ability to put it all together and be good wherever the fight goes is what's helped him to an undefeated professional record that includes wins over the aforementioned Nogueira and Lesnar, as well as guys such as Cheick Kongo and former IFL Heavyweight Champion Ben Rothwell.

However, at a solid 245 pounds in a division that is seeing fighters who have to cut weight to make the 265-pound limit, some critics say the champ may need to put on some weight to compete with other top heavyweights like Carwin, Mir, or Strikeforce champion Alistair Overeem.

Cain disagrees.

"No, I think I've trained and competed with enough guys at that weight that I'm comfortable with it. I've chosen to fight and compete at this weight. And you know, I pretty much have to do it. I think this is as big as I'm gonna get. I can't get any bigger. I've tried, it doesn't work. So this is what I'm gonna train at and fight at."

UFC fighter Kurt Pellegrino told me that when he started his MMA career, he set a goal to become a UFC fighter. Now that he's reached that goal, and has had a successful and lucrative career in the UFC, he wishes that he had reached higher.

"I wish I had said that I wanted to be a UFC champion, because I'm kind of satisfied, and if I retired tomorrow, I wouldn't feel like anything was missing," he said. I ask Cain where he set his goals.

"To be the UFC heavyweight champion. That's the only reason I got into this sport: to be the best. I feel if I hadn't got that belt in my road, in my whole lifetime, I think my career would have been mediocre."

After Welterweight Champion Georges St-Pierre beat Dan Hardy at UFC 111 in Newark, New Jersey, fans and media began to criticize his fighting style, which had become dominated by wrestling. People began to say he was fighting not to lose, as opposed to fighting to win and putting on boring fights in the process (GSP has since destroyed Velasquez teammate Koscheck with a striking exhibition at UFC 124).

I asked Cain if the criticism was justified.

"The fans want to see knockouts," he says. "That's the exciting stuff. People who are well-educated in the sport, they want to see everything: the great wrestling, the great control on the ground, submission attempts, ground and pound, all that stuff. But [everyday] fans want to see knockouts."

While Cain has had the right stuff to win the belt and keep the fans entertained, as well as becoming the only fighter to finish both Lesnar and Nogueira in the process, I wonder if he thinks there's a guy out there who will be able to give him a run for his money.

"Yeah, I think so. When that guy comes, definitely that's why I have my coaches. That's why I always get all my coaches together. We all watch the tape on one guy and we keep watching film until we get a great game plan. We see what he does well. We see what we think our best game would be for that type of fighter."

One of my favorite questions to ask fighters is, "When do you know that you've broken your opponent?" Cain's answer is not unlike others.

"You just see it. He moves slower; you taste blood. You just know when he's starting to break, and then that's when you turn it up. That's when he's pretty much done."

———

When I interviewed Cain shortly before his bout with Lesnar, he was completely at ease and confident in his ability to beat him. It was as if he was salivating for his chance to make an example out of the giant wrestler.

"I'm better in the stand-up. I've wrestled guys bigger than him," he said with steely calm. "I have better hands. I'm faster in takedowns and I know how to scramble if he takes me down. I wasn't that impressed with his Carwin submission, and I know how to get out of those bad positions if it comes to that."

Sensing a bit of anger from the future champ, I changed the subject to his engagement, asking who picked out the ring.

"We kind of both did," he said, lightening up for the first time in the interview. I wasn't sure if he was happy to be discussing his future wife, or if he was just happy to talk about anything but fighting.

"She told me what kind of setting she wanted and I did the rest. I got the diamond over in Los Angeles—the diamond district—and then I got the setting and everything here in San Jose. At that time I was training, so I didn't really have my mind in it as far as what the ring was gonna look like. Then when I saw the ring, I was like, 'Whoa, this is really nice,' and it was definitely a good feeling. But then again, I was training, so it was kind of, 'I definitely gotta win first, and then we can celebrate.'"

With all the hype that surrounded Cain Velasquez leading up to the championship bout against Lesnar and all of the expectations from the Latino community—including a documentary directed by Bobby Razak featuring Cain, Gilbert Melendez, and former WEC bantamweight champ Miguel Torres—having a good woman by his side that can keep him grounded was extremely important.

"She definitely keeps me in my place. She knows that kind of stuff can't get to my head. So she'll say stuff to keep me in place, definitely. I'm not the type of guy to get too big headed or anything like that. But having those kinds of people around definitely helps me. She's always teaching me to be a better man. Whatever kind of day I have in training, I could have the worst day of my life in training and then when I go home I'm gonna have nothing but smiles and hugs. So it's always good."

Cain and his fiancée had a baby girl in 2010, and when I bring her up, he cuts me off, sensing my question.

"As far as people asking, 'Do you have new motivation?' No, I've always had that motivation there. But now I definitely want my kids and my fiancée to have everything that I can give them. Everything that they would want."

Keeping a level head is a good philosophy for any professional athlete, particularly in MMA. Our interview took place not long after heavyweight legend Fedor Emelianenko tapped out for the first time in his professional career, having been caught in a triangle choke by Fabricio Werdum. After one loss people began to call him a fraud, something that Cain thought was unfair to the legendary Russian.

"It definitely is [unfair]. I think what it is, is when you're winning, you're on top, everybody's behind you. Then once you lose, people just push you aside, get somebody else up there. That's the way people are."

Cain has no delusions of keeping his belt forever. He knows that eventually someone will come along who will give him a tough time inside the Octagon.

"I'm not afraid of that," he said. "Definitely, I know everybody loses at one point or another. That happens, definitely happens. But the only things you can do are train hard in here and do as much to try to stop that from happening. I think it all depends on how well you can come back and regroup yourself. You know, if you can show that you learned from your mistakes in the past and that you're a new, different kind of fighter."

CHAPTER 9

MATT HUGHES,
UFC HALL OF FAMER

UFC welterweight Matt Hughes has proven he's the best of the best, time and time again. A two-time UFC champion and a two-time All-American wrestler at Eastern Illinois University, the Illinois farm boy is one of the most decorated fighters in MMA history.

Hughes is a guy I've interviewed at every turn of his career. When I first started covering the UFC in 2001, Hughes was on a tear, defending his welterweight title with some of the most exciting fights in the company's history.

His bouts against Carlos Newton and Frank Trigg are highlight reel battles, even today. But Hughes is easy to misunderstand. I hear people say he's standoffish with the fans. I hear other media professionals say that he's a tough interview. And I hear fighters say he likes to keep to himself. Even Dana White said in Chapter One of this book that he and Hughes had to have a private chat before coming to terms with one another's personalities.

All of this is true. But Hughes is basically a shy guy who fought to the top of a sport that has exploded in popularity, and that's something that I believe Hughes is still coming to terms with. With his level of success in a sport that is now a pop-culture phenomenon, fame comes with the territory, but it's not something Hughes signed up for. To him, it's always been about the fights.

"Some of the best times I ever had were early in the sport when I was going around and fighting with Jeremy Horn, Jens Pulver, my brother, and Pat Miletich, and that's what we did," says Hughes. "It wasn't about money. We lived around each other, we trained together, and we fought together. Those were the fun times."

As Matt's profile rose with the sport, his success inside the Octagon created more of a demand for his time and energy outside of it, both as a celebrity and a voice for the industry. And Hughes lost a lot of the joy of pure competition.

"It became a job after I won the belt," says Hughes. "People started to notice me. I started doing the autographs and pictures, and after I won the belt I didn't have any of my buddies fighting with me on the same card and that was hard. Before, when Jens Pulver or Jeremy Horn were on the card, I really felt lucky because I had more corner-men there and more friends there. But after I won the belt it became more of a job." He even admits that before his championship run at welter-weight he was thinking about a different life for himself.

> **66** Before that first championship fight I made the decision that if I lost to Carlos Newton I was going to walk away. I was going to find a nine-to-fiver, maybe do something with my hands, but I ended up winning the fight and it changed my life. **99**

That was November 2, 2001. It would be nearly three years and five title defenses before he lost his belt to BJ Penn, only to regain it in a victory over Georges St-Pierre after Penn vacated the title to fight in Japan. Hughes then went on to defend the title four more times, including a win in a rematch with Penn before losing the belt to St-Pierre. When he beat Royce Gracie with a first-round TKO after dominating the Brazilian Jiu-Jitsu and UFC legend with superior wrestling, he proved to the world that the sport of MMA had evolved past its founders' dominance on the mat.

In Abu Dhabi at UFC 112 in April of 2010, before taking on Brazilian Jiu-Jitsu legend Renzo Gracie (Royce's cousin), I observed Hughes sitting by himself while waiting for the shuttle to take him to the arena from the hotel. Just 15 feet away stood Renzo with an entourage of about 15 people. The two acknowledged one another, with the affable Gracie walking over to say hello and shake Hughes' hand before retreating back to his group.

As I watched, I couldn't help but wonder what was going through Hughes' mind. He didn't look uncomfortable sitting alone in enemy territory. In all honesty, if I didn't know better, I would have thought he was there to corner another fighter. He didn't seem like he was there to fight at all.

What I saw was a guy who'd been there and done it all before. To Hughes it was just another day at the office, and my guess was that he was tired from the 15 hour flight and from the weight cut. But that night, even after so many years and so many wins, he proved that he was not tired of the game. He finished Renzo with devastating leg kicks and a ground and pound that the 43-year-old Brazilian just wasn't ready for.

By November 2010, Hughes had amassed a professional record of 45 wins and just eight losses. It was an exclamation point on a career resurgence that began with the defeat of Matt Serra in May 2009, and continued with impressive victories against Renzo Gracie and Brazilian Jiu-Jitsu ace, and Renzo protégé, Ricardo Almeida at UFC 117.

It would have been a great finish to the year for Hughes, but then Dana White called him with an offer he couldn't refuse: a rubber match with BJ Penn.

Penn had just come off two consecutive losses to new lightweight champion Frankie Edgar, and many industry insiders believed the rubber match with Hughes would be the Hawaiian's swan's song. Penn, however, had other plans.

Hughes suffered a devastating 21-second TKO loss to Penn at 170 pounds at UFC 123 in Detroit on November 20, 2010, leaving Hughes once again with doubts as to where his future in fighting lay.

"I really don't know what comes next," he told UFC announcer Joe Rogan just after the fight.

It wouldn't be the first time he contemplated his future in fighting. In fact, just a few years ago, the then 35-year-old thought about retirement after verbally submitting at UFC 79 in a bout with Georges St-Pierre. He was dominated by the Canadian at every level of the fight. Afterwards, a battered Hughes told me he needed to go home and re-evaluate his career after taking some time off to hunt white-tailed deer.

If you watch that interview today, you'd probably come to the same conclusion I did that night, which was that Hughes' fighting days were over.

As it turned out, even Hughes himself didn't know just how much he had left in the tank. If things continue to progress in the manner they have, in spite of that loss to Penn, Hughes could end up being the next Randy Couture, fighting at the highest level of the sport well into his forties.

"I'm just taking things one fight at a time," says Hughes. "But the one thing about it is I still love competing. I love being in there. I love the training, so why not? If I ever feel like I don't want to be in there or I don't want to compete, then that'll be the time to walk away."

Hughes has fought the best fighters in the sport throughout his career, and he's beaten the best fighters in the sport throughout his career: Georges St-Pierre in their first meeting inside the Octagon, former champs such as BJ Penn, Matt Serra, Renzo Gracie, and Carlos Newton, as well as young contenders like Thiago Alves and Ricardo Almeida. However, this feat is not something he thinks too much about.

"Now that you say it, looking back, I've always fought the toughest guys, Matt Serra was a former champ, BJ Penn—but to me it's just another day, another opponent, another day in the Octagon and a way for me to provide for my family."

Up to 2010, Hughes had the most title defenses in UFC history with nine. He is a member of the UFC Hall of Fame, and was one of the first really big pay-per-view draws for the company. Matt Hughes is a legend in mixed martial arts and says he's accomplished everything he's set out to do.

"I've never been that guy to chase records. Yeah, I'm a nine-time world champion, but it's only a matter of time before someone comes around and takes that away from me. I realize that. I don't chase records, I just happen to be good at what I do, I happen to enjoy it, and I'll continue like that."

In comparing Hughes to Randy Couture, a fellow wrestler and elder statesmen in the sport, I asked him if being older gives them an advantage over opponents because of experience in the Octagon.

> **"** Oh, I don't know about that. I think whoever is older is at a disadvantage. It takes me longer to prepare. It takes me longer to get through my injuries. It takes longer for the bruises to go away. The only positive would be the experience. I've been in a lot of situations and I don't get rattled out there as easy as I used to, but I'd much rather be that 28-year-old guy full of gumption who doesn't know how to lose, than the older guy like me who picks his battles, picks his situations, and goes with it. I'd love to see the 28-year-old Matt Hughes fight the GSP of today. I think that would be very interesting. Back then I didn't know that I could lose in that many ways. Back then I was very athletic and making people do what I wanted to do. And now I'm comfortable on my back. It doesn't bother me when I'm taken down; a lot has changed. **"**

"I think I relied a lot on my wrestling skills. I think that won a lot of matches for me. I think that still wins matches for me. That's what I credit my Royce Gracie win to, my American wrestling. I was able to control him. He wasn't used to that. I was so young and so athletic I was able to do what I wanted to do. People didn't have the strength or athleticism to keep up with me. It was a fun game. Go in, beat somebody up."

But even Hughes concedes that while his victory over Royce was a passing of the torch in some sense, mixed martial arts is a sport that is constantly evolving.

"Back when I started you could be one dimensional. I was a wrestler who knew some submissions but with very limited stand-up," he says. "But I could beat people because if somebody was close enough to punch me I was close enough to take him down. And when I got him down I was so strong and I knew how to stay out of bad situations and I could beat him. But now, it's not that way anymore. You have to be top at everything. You've got to know striking, wrestling, and submissions. You have to know everything and if you don't know them all, somebody's going to exploit it."

Hughes learned that firsthand in his two losses to Georges St-Pierre, who is widely considered the best all-around fighter in the business. Rich Franklin learned that in his two fights against Anderson Silva. BJ Penn learned that in his two losses to Frankie Edgar, and Brock Lesnar learned that against Cain Velasquez. It just goes to show you that MMA is a sport where anyone can lose, any time.

"GSP is on top of the world, no doubt about it. His wrestling is very good, and what I think GSP does a really good job with is his transitions. He can transition from striking to wrestling very quick, and disguise it so people don't see it. That's one of his best wrestling qualities, his transitions," says Hughes, who knows wrestling as well as anybody in the sport.

———

> "Us fighters know that it's a chess match out there. To every move there's a counter, and to every counter there's a counter, so I have to watch to see what my opponent's doing. He could be setting something up two and three moves down the line, where you move your hand and suddenly you're in a submission, so we realize that it's a chess match, and a lot of [people] don't realize how much strategy there is out there. "

One of the most frustrating things for fighters, promoters, and educated fans of mixed martial arts is the state of judging. Many decisions just go horribly wrong, giving birth to one of the most used clichés in the sport: "Never leave it to the judges."

"I don't have any complaints with the refs," says Hughes. "I can disagree. When someone has side control and is landing effective strikes I don't agree with standing them up. If he's doing effective striking let him stay down there. He's doing what you've got to do. I do have issues with the judges. We need quality judges in there, and without that it's going to be hard to move the sport forward. I don't have a problem with the scoring system. I just don't know where some of these judges come up with their criteria for judging. My first criteria has always been, who did the most damage in the round? From there it goes aggressiveness, technique, and who had the most control, but I'm a damage guy. For me that's the whole point of being in there. I don't know how to fix it. I just know it needs to be fixed."

Hughes grew up around farm work and wrestling. You know that expression "farm strength"? It's not just an expression. Matt Hughes has farm strength. He's the type of wrestler who can keep anyone on the mat through sheer brute force.

"What made me who I am today is the fact that I have a twin brother, and that brought competition into my life very early," Hughes explains. "The second thing is growing up on the farm. With the farm work I always had something to do, and I learned competition and work ethic early on, and that's stayed with me and I think that's what made me successful today."

Many MMA greats have brothers who also train in the sport or who are very competitive athletically. Clay Guida wouldn't be one of the most exciting fighters in the UFC if his older brother Jason didn't first try MMA. Jon Jones has one brother in the NFL and another who is NFL bound. Matt Hughes has a twin brother named Mark, and together they tore up the house and the farm, but Mark took a different path in life.

"My brother was always the type of guy who, when he would wrestle he would go through his opponent," says Hughes. "He was going to outmuscle him. And when it would come to somebody who had his strength but more technique he'd lose. So Mark got to the point where he was going to really have to start training to compete in the sport, and he elected not to."

Hughes has a son from his first marriage and two daughters in his second marriage with his wife, Audra, who also has a son from a previous marriage. He talks about how they met in his autobiography *Made In America: The Most Dominant Champion in UFC History*, and he told me how she deals with his career.

"I've known my wife forever and I was wrestling in high school, in college, when I first started to get to know her, and she knows that's who I am. She's all right with it, but she gets nervous.

"When I fought with Frank Trigg the first time he got on top of me and was throwing some punches, and she got so nervous she ran from the bottom of the arena all the way to the top, and by the time she got to the top she turned around and saw that I was on top of Trigg, so she ran all the way back down to the bottom again. It's an emotional rollercoaster for her. I can relate to that.

"When I have a good friend like Robbie Lawler or my brother fighting in the Octagon, it's hard on me. When I'm on the outside coaching somebody, I'd rather be inside the Octagon fighting than outside where

I can't do anything. I've always said it's harder on the cornermen than the guy fighting. When you're cornering you don't know if your fighter is hearing you. You're trying to yell out the right things, but you can't do anything. I'm outside the cage and that's not who I am. When my buddies are going through a hard time I'm right next to him most of the time. With the cage between us I can't do that."

Balancing a family and a career as a fighter is probably the hardest thing to do, especially hard for the guys in the Hughes and Couture era. When guys are training wrestling at the level these guys did, during the time when MMA didn't exist, the Olympics were the end-all, be-all. Conventional wisdom about getting to the Olympics is that one has to give up everything and isolate one's self and just train, train, train.

Wrestlers before MMA were like that as well, because when it came to combat sports, it was the Marines. Not even boxing could compare to the amount of sacrifice it takes to be a dominant wrestler in the elite status of the sport. It's a constant battle with dieting, training, lifting, and cardio.

Nowadays wrestlers know there is a sport that's even harder to train for, and that's MMA, so their attitude is much different. Wrestlers are no longer the toughest guys on the mat.

"Early in my career it was easy because I lived by myself," says Hughes. "I woke up and I trained. I'd come home and think about training, and then go back to train, throw some food somewhere in there, and that was it. Now I've got four kids, a wife, and it's just not as easy to get those good meals in, the rest you need with a newborn kid is hard to come by, and getting away to go train because I want to spend time with my family is more difficult, so it's a lot more complicated than it used to be."

I see younger guys in Hughes' position handle the life better because for them, training is their job. Frankie Edgar doesn't have to work as a plumber on the side to pay the bills. One has to understand, when guys like Couture and Hughes were coming up, making a living solely as a fighter was impossible. The money just wasn't there. And even though both Hughes and Couture have made millions of dollars fighting, it's hard to change that "nobody understands what I have to go through," mentality.

Now that Couture has found success in movies, I've noticed a much different person than I interviewed back in 2001. Randy Couture is so much more comfortable in his own skin. He's slain the dragons. He's content and he knows he's got nothing more to prove. Hughes is getting there, but remember, Randy's 10 years older than Hughes.

Some guys, however, weren't so fortunate when it came to the fame and money some of the top MMA guys get today. Even Hughes' first MMA coach, Pat Miletich, who nowadays is a respected commentator and analyst, didn't achieve the amount of success that he should have (read Jon Wertheim's *Blood In The Cage* for the complete Miletich story).

Pat Miletich created the Miletich Fighting System (MFS) in sleepy Bettendorf, Iowa, back in the early 1990s. At the time, Ken Shamrock's Lion's Den in Susanville, California, was the only other place to go to get real MMA training, and Miletich churned out not only Matt Hughes, but Jens Pulver, Tim Sylvia, Jeremy Horn, and countless others. Pat himself was the first UFC welterweight champion, winning the belt in 1998.

> **"**I look up to Pat Miletich. He's a great guy," says Hughes. "We don't talk as much anymore, but with that guy, let me tell you, he was hard to spar with, he was hard to wrestle with, and he was hard to grapple with. He was very well-rounded and I think he doesn't get the credit he should in this sport. He's a pioneer. I would put Pat against GSP, because I'd love to see the matchup. I'd love to see what happens. I'd love to see GSP try striking with him, which would be awesome. But I look up to Pat. He's on top of the list. **"**

Miletich was unceremoniously erased from the official UFC history books, but I believe it's only a matter of time before whatever personal issues there are will be resolved and Miletich will take his proper place in the annals of UFC history. He wouldn't be the first guy to have issues with the UFC brass, and I asked Hughes how he avoided all of the drama a lot of his peers, like Randy Couture and Tito Ortiz, could not.

Both of those champion fighters held out for better contracts, and even though things worked out, there was a lot of bad blood that flowed between Dana White and those two during the process.

"Tito is Tito, and I think he's made some bad decisions. Randy, I just don't know," says Hughes. "Dana White and I are extremely good friends. He's a boss, a friend, and like a father. If I need something I can call Dana White and he'll help me out. I think Dana is really misunderstood. When he walks into an arena it takes him an hour to get to the cage. He is the best about being with the fans, signing autographs, taking pictures. I've seen guys say, 'We came down from Canada just to see the sport,' and he'll get them better tickets. Dana's the best. When it comes to talking with the public, being friendly and doing what the public wants, he's the best."

Matt Hughes doesn't like to watch his fights. It's certainly not unique. Many actors can't watch themselves on the screen, and many interviewers have a difficult time watching themselves conduct interviews.

"When I was a titleholder I used to watch just to hear what the commentators had to say, but I can't tell you the last time I watched one of my fights. It would have to be years ago."

At the end of the interview I ask him if he has any regrets.

"I think everybody's got regrets. When it comes to fighting I don't have many, but sure, I could have trained harder for some people. I could have done things different in the Octagon. But for the most part I'm pretty happy. I do contemplate retiring but then I go back to this is what I do, and this is what I love. There are a lot of people who don't want to wake up and go to work every day. I think there are more people who don't want to go to work than who do. Right now I still enjoy working. I still enjoy working out. I like to travel; I provide pretty well for my family."

Whether or not Matt Hughes will ever be satisfied with his legacy is anyone's guess. He says he doesn't like the word *legacy*, that fighting is just a sport. But he's wrong there. MMA is a cultural phenomenon, and when Hughes is an old man it may very well be as big as the NFL. And when his great-grandchildren are gathered to watch the Super Bowl of MMA on television, he will have been one of the men who paved the way.

CHAPTER 10

SCOTT COKER, STRIKEFORCE FOUNDER AND CEO

In March of 2011, Coker shocked the MMA world when he agreed to be bought out by the UFC for an undisclosed sum of money, taking a salary to run the Strikeforce promotion under the Zuffa banner.

This interview was conducted prior to the finalized sale, and has not been altered.

———

Strikeforce CEO and Founder Scott Coker has built a career as a martial arts promoter dating back to the early days of ESPN.

It was Coker who produced the PKA (Professional Karate Association) fights on the fledgling all sports network, making guys like Don "The Dragon" Wilson and Cliff Thomas famous among the martial arts faithful. Later he put K1 on ESPN2 after becoming the Japanese kickboxing organization's head of U.S. operations. Fights were held at the Bellagio in Las Vegas, where he made early MMA star Frank Shamrock and a little-known *Sanshou* fighter named Cung Le two of his headliners. In the '90s he founded Strikeforce as a kickboxing promotion in San Jose, and when the state of California finally legalized mixed martial arts in 2006, it was Scott Coker who filled the HP Pavilion with what was, at the time, a U.S. record for a live, paying audience for a mixed martial arts event.

After acquiring well-known fighters such as Kimbo Slice from the now-shuttered EliteXC (ProElite), Coker negotiated a deal with Showtime that has kept mixed martial arts on premium cable. He also created a separate deal with CBS that saw Russian legend Fedor Emelianenko fight on network television for the first time—knocking out previously unbeaten heavyweight Brett Rogers.

Strikeforce is also the largest promotion to award belts in women's mixed martial arts, giving Cristiane "Cyborg" Santos the 145 pound strap after she beat down Gina Carano in a fight that also aired on CBS.

Coker made headlines in early 2011 by announcing a heavyweight tournament that would include Fedor, K1 and Strikeforce champ Alistair Overeem, Fabricio Werdum, and Antonio "Bigfoot" Silva in the brackets.

Scott Coker is an accomplished promoter who is happy with his place in MMA. He doesn't mind being caught in the shadow that the UFC casts over the industry, believing there's room for everybody to put on great shows and make money in the process. Though, like any company that expands from a regional base to a national one, there were growing pains for the Northern California MMA league when it found itself suddenly competing with the UFC for eyeballs and talent.

"It's been phenomenal," says Coker. "Before the acquisition of ProElite, we were really a regional show, mostly in the [San Francisco] Bay Area. And as you know, now it's a national show, traveling all over the country and doing well. So it's exciting. I think there were definitely some adjustments that needed to be made. We were doing four fights a year in 2006, 2007, and 2008. This year we're going up to 20 fights in a calendar year between March 1st and March 1st the following year, so it's been an expansion process, a staffing process. It's been a learning process, but it's good."

Just as UFC president Dana White credits guys like Chuck Liddell, Randy Couture, Ken Shamrock, and Royce Gracie for helping to build the UFC (all of whom are UFC Hall of Famers), Coker says there are four guys who've helped build Strikeforce as well.

"When I think about the four fighters that were really the foundation, the building blocks of Strikeforce, it was Frank Shamrock, who had a career, obviously way before he fought for us," says Coker. "Then it's Cung Le. We started promoting Cung Le as a *Sanshou* fighter here in town in 1997. So it's been a long time. Then, when I think about the other two fighters, it's Josh Thomson and Gilbert Melendez. Josh was a guy that came over from UFC when they had cut out their lightweight division at that time, and Gilbert was a fighter that Javier Mendez said to me, 'You've got to take a look at this guy and you've got to grab him.' Really, he was the first guy that I think we took from ground zero, so to speak, from our league and built him all the way to become the superstar that he is today."

Before he founded Strikeforce, Coker was the PKA producer on ESPN. His first broadcast was in 1985 in San Jose's Civic Auditorium.

"It's a small building, holds like 3,000 people. The league—the Professional Karate Association (PKA)—was all above-the-waist kickboxing. So it didn't have any leg kicks, no elbows, it wasn't like Thai boxing. It was the formation before Thai boxing became popular. There was another league called WKA but our alliance was with PKA. They would roll into town, we would produce the live events, and it would be shown on ESPN. So our relationship with ESPN started back in 1985. And the first fight, for the people that remember back in the day, it was "Bad" Brad Hefton and a guy named Don Nealson. But we promoted Don Wilson, Cliff Thomas, Felipe Garcia, Alvin Prouder, all the guys that were popular in the '80s in the kickboxing circuit, except for Bill Wallace. Bill had just retired when I first started getting into the scene. He had his last fight and I think it was on CBS. Benny Urquidez was just having his last fight, so it was kind of at the end of that era that I got into the martial arts fight business. So we did fights for ESPN, and back then they didn't have any major league sports. ESPN was more Australian Rules Football and a bunch of late night reruns. But they loved martial arts. So they had a good thing going with PKA. We were one of the promoters among the circuit in the U.S. Then, when ESPN2 launched, we got a call directly from ESPN saying they'd like to continue martial arts because it was a good ratings deliverer for [the original] ESPN. 'We're launching ESPN2,' they said. I believe it was '93. And they were looking for programming that would complement their extreme motorcycle racing."

Recognizing an opportunity when presented with one, Coker started his own kickboxing promotion called Strikeforce to offer programming to ESPN2.

"I think we did 20 hours a year for them, plus reruns. So it was airing all the time. We did some amazing fights here in town. We did some amazing fights overseas. We were the first U.S. broadcast team to go to Bangkok and we filmed in Lumpini Stadium. So it was great coverage and it was good for us."

But Strikeforce was put on the back burner when Coker received a call from Japan. K1 founder Mr. Ishii wanted a meeting.

"They had reached out to me, saying, 'We want you to come to Japan and take a meeting with Mr. Ishii. We would like to have you do shows for us in Las Vegas.' And my initial response was, you know, I really don't want to do it because in America at that time, really no one knew what K1 was. Plus, I felt like we had a good thing going. We had a TV deal. We were growing off some sponsorships. We had some great fighters. And it was kind of on its way."

Reluctantly, Coker took the trip to Japan to meet the famed kickboxing promoter.

"I went to Japan and watched the fights," Coker says. "To see K1 and to see how big they are over there at that time, they were massive, doing arena shows. I don't mean arena shows like HP Pavilion with 18,000–20,000 seats. We're talking baseball stadiums, Tokyo Dome, Nagoya Dome, Fukuoka Dome. They were doing dome tours at that time, and it was massive. It was impressive. Mr. Ishii lured me in and made me a very, very good deal, and I felt that it was the right move."

Scott said being in a dome packed with tens of thousands of fans watching kickboxing was an experience he'll never forget.

"You know, unless you've been there to see it, there's nothing like it in the world. I think the average ticket price is right around $100, $125, so in their heyday, they were doing extremely well. And they had a great TV deal. They still have a TV deal, but they had a great TV deal back then. They were packing the stadiums. They had big stars. This was when Ernesto Hoost was still in his prime. Even when Bob Sapp came, I remember going to Tokyo where there was 70,000 people, and you walk in and you're just like, 'This is unbelievable.'"

In 2004, Coker heard rumblings about the California State Athletic Commission thinking about sanctioning mixed martial arts, and he started making moves to be ready to go as soon as that decision was made. He went to one of the most famous MMA fighters he knew and locked him into a contract to fight on his card, if in fact there would be one.

"Frank Shamrock and I had been friends for a long time, and there had been information here that the state of California was going to legalize mixed martial arts. So I sat down with Frank and said, 'This is something that if they're going to do it, meaning the state, I want to be the first promoter and I want you to come fight for me. Come out of retirement and come fight for me.' So he said okay, and he and I entered into a contract in 2004. But it took over a year and a half from there for it to become legal, not until March 2006. They just kept extending it, extending it. And at one point I just felt like, 'It's not going to happen. They're just not going to do it.' I was still working for K1, so I was just kind of going about my business, throwing the fights in Las Vegas for K1. So when they pulled the trigger, I got the call from [former commissioner] Armando Garcia saying, 'We're going to do this.' I said, 'Armando, you know, I've been a promoter here for 22 years. I've had a longest consecutive promoter license in the state for anybody here in mixed martial arts. You have to give it to me.' So, he said, 'Yeah, I'll give it to you, because you deserve to have it.'

———

> ❝So I was thankful to him for that. And then we threw the first fight here in San Jose, I remember setting up the scale in the arena and going, 'Well, I don't know how many people are going to come. Maybe 6,000 or 7,000 people? But I really don't know.' So we set it up for about 8,000 people. And then we started selling and selling and it just kind of grew. We had 18,265, and it's still the record for paid attendance in the United States. For me, it's a historical moment in my martial arts promoting career, and I think it's a historical moment for mixed martial arts. I'd think for Frank and Cung and those guys that helped launch Strikeforce, that it was a magic moment for them as well. ❞

The growth of Strikeforce and Coker's experience dealing with Japanese promoters has led to co-promotions with Tokyo-based Fighting Entertainment Group, which owns Dream. For instance, Dream Lightweight Champion Shinya Aoki fought Strikeforce Lightweight Champion Gilbert Melendez in 2010, dropping a unanimous decision. Then Strikeforce Heavyweight Champion Alistair Overeem took on Todd Duffee at Dream's annual Dynamite New Year's Eve show at Saitama Arena. The Reem KO'd Duffee in just 19 seconds.

That said, Coker doesn't see Strikeforce expanding internationally as quickly as the UFC has.

"I think we have a lot of work here. I think we're going to focus our efforts here and grow the brand here because we have a lot of work to do. Maybe that's something that 18 months or two years from now we can have a better grasp on."

While the UFC used a reality show, *The Ultimate Fighter*, which airs on SpikeTV, to cultivate new talent and resurrect old fighters as coaches, Strikeforce has the Showtime *Challenger* series to do the same.

"The *Challenger* show really is for up-and-coming talent," says Coker. "Sometimes we'll put in fighters that maybe have had their day and are trying to resurrect their career, and what we'll do is we'll put the young guy against the veteran guy, and if the veteran guy can win then maybe he'll work his way back up. Like the Mike Kyle situation. Since he lost to Fabricio Werdum he's won five fights in a row. So we let him fight outside of Strikeforce, we put him in the *Challengers*, let him build his way back up. He beat Feijao in St. Louis last year. So he's working his way back up. So that's one way. The other *Challenger* scenario is a guy like Luke Rockhold or a guy like Tyrone Woodley or [female standout] Sarah Kaufman, fighters that aren't really that known yet. You know, you give these guys an opportunity to fight, to get on national TV and start building their fan base at an early age. We put some tough fights on *Challenger*, because it's not the [type of] league that we're just going build this guy. We're going to test these guys. It's a proving ground for the young talent for Strikeforce and I think Woodley, and Rockhold, and Kaufman, I think they've proven now that they can take the job to the big fight. So, those three will have graduated to the big fight this year. But it took about a year to develop them and get them ready."

Strikeforce had two high-profile rookies, NFL legend Herschel Walker and TNA wrestler Bobby Lashley, fight in its big shows. Coker has taken some criticism for those decisions. In Walker's case, he was making his professional MMA debut on a main card, at 47 years of age. He won. Lashley, on the other hand, has been spoon-fed opponents and has heard criticism that he's ducking proper talent.

Coker explains.

"The thing with Bobby is he's a fighter. He'll probably fight any-body. But the problem is, if we throw him in there too fast, then it'll be, 'Oh, you guys ruined his career. You should have given him more tune-up fights. You should've given him this.' I think there's a pro-gression of fights that he should have, that we feel we're going to give him. But each way he's going to get tested. And if he doesn't graduate to the next level, so to speak, then maybe he shouldn't fight at that level. For us to throw him into a Fedor fight, an Alistair Overeem fight, something that I feel is over his head right now—that's just my opinion, because he'll feel differently—he'll probably say, 'I'll fight anybody.' But his management and our company are congruent and have the same feeling about where he is headed. Because this guy, today, I think he's a good fighter. Give him eight to 10 fights, what's he going to be like a year from now, 18 months from now? The guy's athletic, he's a physical specimen, strong. You know, he can wrestle, and now he's learning his striking. I think he's at AKA [American Kickboxing Academy] learning it right now. You know, what could he be in 18 months? And that's really what my vision is. It's not today. It's 12–18 months from now. Then he can fight those big fights and be competitive."

A few weeks after this interview was taped, however, Coker expressed some dissatisfaction with Lashley after a poor performance against Chad Griggs. Lashley failed to answer the bell for the third round and was rushed to the hospital after suffering dehydration and exhaustion.

"We'll be talking to Bobby later," Coker said at the postfight press conference. "You know he's going to have to do some soul searching and really decide what he wants to do."

As for Walker, while most MMA fans originally believed he was way too old to be fighting, he won his first fight in convincing fashion, defeating Greg Nagy via TKO due to strikes. He also trains very hard and applies himself in the gym, training alongside guys like Cain Velasquez and Dan Cormier at AKA.

"Herschel's a superstar everywhere he goes," Scott says.

Speaking of Cormier, Walker was forced to pull out of his second appearance inside the cage, scheduled for December 2010, after the former Olympic gold medalist kneed him in training, causing a bad cut.

"I feel terrible about this," Walker said via a press release. "I know things like this happen in all sports, but I had trained very hard and was excited to be returning to the cage again. I hope to fight again as soon as the cut heals." (Walker would go on to defeat Scott Carson by TKO at 3:13 of Round 1, on January 29, 2011.)

———

Strikeforce and M1 Global—a company that not only promotes MMA but also serves as management for Fedor Emelianenko—came to an agreement to co-promote fights in which Fedor would fight in the main event. When Fedor lost his first professional bout in summer 2010 against Brazilian Jiu-Jitsu ace Fabricio Werdum, it was his first loss in a decade. Coker watched that match cageside.

> ❝Fedor is a phenomenon," Coker says. "I watched him fight for all those years in Japan when I was working there, and for me to see the loss—I'm sure it was devastating for him—but it was sad for me as well, from a fan perspective. But I think for a company it's good because now we have so many great heavyweights in Strikeforce. And now the deck gets reshuffled and now you think about it, Fabricio Werdum can fight Alistair Overeem in the rematch, right? Alistair Overeem could fight Fedor, Fedor could fight Werdum again. Then you put Kharitonov in that mix, you put in "Big Foot" Silva against Fedor. That's not a gimme fight. That fight could go either way. We just have so many great heavyweights right now that the possibilities of the matchups are exciting. ❞

Of course, whenever any journalist like me talks to Scott Coker, the elephant in the room will always be the UFC. When it comes to mixed martial arts, the UFC is the pound-for-pound No. 1 organization in the world. They acquired Japan's Pride FC when fans clamored loud enough about making super-fights between UFC guys like Randy Couture and Chuck Liddell versus Pride fighters like Wanderlei Silva and Mirko "Cro Cop" Filipovic.

When the upstart WEC secured a broadcast deal with the Versus network, the UFC was smart enough to recognize an opportunity and purchased the promotion, securing marketshare among young male driven cable channels, such as SpikeTV. In 2010, Zuffa got rid of the WEC altogether, creating two more weight classes in the UFC with an eye toward unifying their two lightweight belts.

It wasn't too many years ago that UFC president Dana White was singing Coker's praises, but that was when Strikeforce was a regional player. The relationship became strained when Strikeforce became a national player with a Showtime and CBS television deal. Like all business, competition creates friction. Coker however, remains unfazed.

"I've said this over and over. When I wake up every day, they're not even on the radar. To me, we have so much work ahead of us, and I'm focusing on Arizona and Houston and other fights that we're doing. I mean, we're monitoring everything, believe me. But some days I just have so much work to do I don't even get a chance to read the trades or the blogs. Maybe once every 10 days I'll be able to get on there. But I have other guys, you know, monitoring everything and responding to things. I'm very happy with where Strikeforce is. We have a great relationship with Showtime. You know, we're so happy to have the relationship with CBS. We're growing at a rate that's—in 18 months, to do the things that we've done and put together the fights that we've put on—it's unheard of.

"I think that's a testament to our staff and also to the knowledge that I've brought to the mixed martial arts game, because it's not like we just got into the business in 2006. So all these other leagues are failing: Affliction, IFL, Bodog, and I'm sure we could probably name others. All those leagues failed because that's not their core business. Well, you know, martial arts fighting has been my core business for 25 years. So that experience comes to the table. When I was working for K1, I learned so much about the international fight business. Mr. Ishii, the owner of K1, I'm very thankful to him. If he ever needed help, I would always help him because he was very good to me. That was like my master's degree program and it basically was getting my education. Now I can do deals with Japan, whereas, if you haven't worked there and you don't know how the culture is and the martial arts environment is, you'll never be able to pull that off. I think UFC tried to do it 2004 or 2005, with Pride. But I'm telling you, unless you really learn the culture and how they operate—and I was on the inside so I have friends in there—and it still took me a year to get that Aoki fight done with Gilbert."

Of course it doesn't hurt that Coker is half-Korean and was born in Seoul.

"Well, you know, here's the one thing I think it did, growing up in Korea for the nine years that I was there, my father was in the import/ export business. My dad was an ex-military guy born and raised in Knoxville, Tennessee. [He] went over there [Korea], met my mom, stayed there for 18 years. But growing up in Asian culture, growing up with a martial arts background, it definitely helped me navigate in the world of Japan and in Korea. Because it's a separate culture, every country has its own culture. But the martial arts fight business, you're dealing with a lot of guys that are martial arts guys. Mr. Ishii was a karate master first before he became head of K1. So there's a certain hierarchy there that I can understand growing up in a martial arts school. I think it's helped me navigate through business over there."

However, just as doing business with Japan has its own idiosyncrasies, so does doing business with Russians. Over the years the relationship between M1 Global and Strikeforce has been strained, to say the least, and MMA critics have been quick to point fingers at Coker or M1 when fights between Fedor and big-name fighters do not come to fruition.

"Again, I think it's a cultural issue," Coker says. "Sometimes it's a translation issue with M1. I get things translated to me, and I go, 'There's no way this could be real.' You know? 'This cannot be real.' And then when I go to another translator I find out, 'No, this means this and this, not what I was thinking,' and then you get through the cultural issue. From what I hear, that's how business is done in Russia. It's different from the United States. So, has it been challenging? Yeah, it's frustrating, because I think Fedor would like nothing more than just to fight. Put him in the cage, let him fight. He'd probably want to fight two or three times a year. But things are good now with M1, so let's just keep it going and let the past be the past. But I think those are the two issues, the cultural barrier and the translation issue."

I steer the conversation back to the competition between the UFC and Strikeforce by bringing up UFC 117, featuring a middleweight title bout between Anderson Silva and Chael Sonnen. The fight takes place in Oakland, California, in Strikeforce's front yard, so to speak.

> "You know, people say, 'Oh, it's you guys against UFC.' But let me tell you, this is how I feel: this is an industry, and no one's going to own the industry even if they want to. You're not going to own martial arts. You're not going to own mixed martial arts. They're a league inside mixed martial arts. We're a league inside mixed martial arts. So is Dream. There are all these different leagues inside mixed martial arts. So they come to town. I think it's good for mixed martial arts as an industry. Because what happens if they came to Oakland and sold 3,000 tickets? That means the industry is not healthy. So to me, let them do their part. Let us do our part. Let Dream do their part. And let's grow this thing. Because you know what, it's not like football. It's not like baseball. It's not like basketball. No matter what they say, it's not at that level yet. I believe it's a niche sport that's growing and has some momentum, but to take it to the real masses? Look at hockey. I go to the stadium downtown and three times a week they're packing 18,000 seats. Three times a week. That's not happening in MMA. It's just not happening. So you know, to me everybody does their part, and when they have success, that's good, and when we have success, that's good."

Coker's many years as a martial arts fight promoter give him a unique perspective on how the business has changed, and where to focus his energy in order to maximize revenue. I ask him what's more important these days, the live gate sales or the television deals.

"When we first started in the martial arts business, back in 1985, it was all a gate business. It was 100 percent gate business, and that stayed that way pretty much until we had the HDNet deal. Then it started changing a little bit. Then, when we created the Showtime relationship, at first I would say it was probably about a 50/50 split. But now, when you look at Strikeforce it's not just television revenue and it's not just the gate. Now there are sponsorships which are pretty sizable. We have great sponsors: Rockstar, Full Tilt Poker, EA Sports, and GoDaddy for the Fedor fight. So then the gate becomes percentage wise, less than it did prior to us having a TV deal because now sponsors are on board. We have a seven-figure international TV deal with Shine International, which is owned by Universal. They handle our international distribution. We have deals in Australia, Italy, the Philippines, I could just go on and on. I think it's like 80 countries now, so that's another revenue stream. And then there's digital downloading and merchandise. So Strikeforce is not just relying on the gate anymore. The gate is really less and less of a percentage of the overall income of the company. But it's always nice to have a million-dollar gate like we did with Fedor or to have just a sizable gate. Because to walk into a building and have 10,000–15,000 people, it just feels good. You feel like this is a great event—it's a big event. And it's exciting because then you get those people screaming and yelling for one guy or the other, and it feels like not *just* a fight. Because to me, there's a fight and then there's an event."

———

When I interviewed former UFC fighter Matt Lindland on *Fighting Words,* he told me that he believes the MMA media shortchanges Strikeforce in favor of UFC coverage.

"I think there's some truth to that," Coker agrees. "When I look at the [heavyweight] ranking, to me, we have the guy that beat the No. 1 guy [Werdum and Fedor respectively]. He should be the No. 1 guy. So there are politics that play into that. But you know what? We're just going to keep on fighting and keep on pushing and driving this bus forward, because eventually we're going to gain that respect from everybody."

After UFC 101 in August 2009, the MMA media, including three of the more prominent combat sports journalists: Yahoo!Sports' Kevin Iole and Steve Cofield, along with Yahoo!Sports Canada's Neil Davidson, peppered Dana White with questions about the announcement that Fedor had signed with Strikeforce, asking why the UFC couldn't get the deal done.

"If I was sitting on Fedor's lap that deal wouldn't have gotten done," White explained. "We went in there to do a deal; they didn't. If you were on this call…it wouldn't have mattered if we flew to Russia and sat in his living room. We weren't getting a deal done that day."

Davidson then remarked to White that he's always been complimentary of Strikeforce, but asked if the gloves were off now that Strikeforce had planned their media conference call regarding the signing of Fedor at the same time the UFC had its own press conference. And did he see it as them (Strikeforce) coming after him? Dana didn't sugarcoat his response.

"They should've stayed the way they were."

Then Cofield, who also posted this entire exchange on his YouTube channel and blog, pressed White by asking if he would consider counter-programming against Strikeforce the way he did when Affliction promoted MMA events.

"We'll see how that goes," White said. "They want to fight me, we're gonna fight. You know how that goes, and you know how that ends."

Dana went on to call Coker's organization Strike Farce, asking who Fedor would actually fight in that league.

Coker responded to White's comments one week later during the conference call announcing the Fedor signing, in which he said: "He's going to go on and say what he's going to say, but we've been in business a long time and I think we know how to operate a business."

Coker recalls the comments on *Fighting Words*.

"You know, when it first happened and I first heard about it I was a little surprised, because we always had a mutually respectful relationship. He was doing his thing and we were doing our thing. I think it changed when we signed Fedor, the temperature changed. Then he started calling us names and disparaging us. You know, to me, he's the front guy. He's the promoter, and he's out there saying things whether they're true or not, because a lot of times he's just barking out facts that have nothing behind them. So to me it's like, you know, I think I've learned to accept it, saying, 'This is just him being a promoter and being out there.'

"To me it's just unnecessary, because we're trying to do our part and grow the industry. But you're not going to hear me saying disparaging things toward him. I mean, I hear all the things—they call us Strike Farce. Well, I've heard people refer to them as U-Farce-C. I've heard UFC stands for U-Fight-Cheap. Frank Shamrock told me that one. But you don't hear me out there barking that stuff. You know what I mean? Why go out there and attack companies? Let me tell you, every manager, every gym owner that wants to be in the fight game wants us to thrive and be their neck-and-neck competitor, because if the UFC was the only one bidding for a fighter, what's going to happen? Then the price of the fighters is going to go down. We're that league that can pay Dan Henderson and Fedor—that can be competitive and make a good future for other fighters."

CHAPTER 11

RANDY COUTURE, UFC HALL OF FAMER

Randy "The Natural" Couture is, along with fellow UFC fighter Chuck Liddell, one of the most famous fighters in the history of mixed martial arts.

A three-time UFC heavyweight champion and two-time UFC light heavyweight champion, Couture has the distinction of being the first fighter to hold the belt in two different weight divisions. He's also, at age 48, the oldest fighter to ever win a UFC bout.

Couture's continued success at such an advanced age in a sport dominated by men in their twenties and early thirties is a constant storyline whether he wins or loses; however, it seems like 2011 will be the year Captain America hangs up his four-ounce gloves for good. With an acting career on the make, and coming off of an easy win in an MMA bout against boxing great James Toney at UFC 118, there's nothing left for him to prove.

One of the sports pioneers, Couture shared an epic trilogy of fights with Liddell (Liddell took two out of three), and famously spanked UFC bad boy Tito Ortiz on the behind during their light heavyweight championship match at UFC 44 in 2003, which Randy won by unanimous decision.

A four-time U.S. Olympic wrestling alternate, an NCAA All-American at Oklahoma State, and a veteran of the U.S. Army, the list of Couture's accomplishments inside and outside of the cage is unmatched by any other fighter in mixed martial arts. An author (*Becoming The Natural* with Loretta Hunt), a UFC and ESPN commentator, an actor who found himself working with Hollywood luminaries such as David Mamet (*Red Belt*) and Sylvester Stallone (*The Expendables*), a TV personality whose commentary is sought after by guys like me looking for a sound bite, and a business owner (Xtreme Couture gyms and clothing lines), it's safe to say Randy Couture has been living the dream.

As Randy mentioned in this book's foreword, I've been interviewing him and covering his career for more than a decade. By the time I interviewed Randy for *Fighting Words* in the fall of 2010, Couture had been divorced three times, saw his son Ryan follow in his footsteps and make his professional MMA debut with Strikeforce, wrote a best-selling autobiography, starred in *The Expendables* and *The Scorpion King*, created a clothing line with Affliction, opened up two world-renowned MMA gyms in two different countries, and created a critically acclaimed fitness regimen now followed by professional athletes in the NFL, MLB, and NBA. And that's not to mention his incredible fighting career.

In other words, the guy's been extremely busy.

"I keep pinching myself," says Couture. "New doors keep opening and new stuff keeps happening. I love my job. I love getting in the cage. I love competing. I like being in the gym, training and working with the guys and learning new skills. It's a lot of fun. I don't have a bucket list. I'm not out to say, 'I really want to do this now.' I'm just having a blast at taking them as they come."

Randy caused quite a stir in the MMA world in December 2010, when he tweeted on his official Twitter timeline the following:

> **"**Thanks to everybody who's been tweeting about seeing my fights. I must have missed the memo. I think I'm at the end of it y'all. It's time. **"**

ESPN.com quickly called and did an interview with him, posting a story on the news site about how Randy was, in fact, not retiring any time soon. That should give an indication on just how popular Couture is, and the impact he's had on the sport.

"I started looking at fighting differently about six, maybe seven years ago," Randy tells me. "You know, we started trying to form Team Quest up in Oregon [with Matt Lindland and Dan Henderson], and look at that as more of a business, instead of just a room where a bunch of guys could work out. And that started my mind-set of looking at brands, looking at logos, looking at all those sorts of things, and changed the way I thought. I began forming business plans and forming a business and LLCs and all that stuff. And up until that point, I hadn't really thought about it. I was getting hammered with taxes, you know, paying self-employment tax and all these things that I didn't really understand or know how to get around. So I think once that vehicle started taking off, I started looking at myself as an athlete and a fighter a little bit differently. And that has kind of blossomed into this whole array of things, clothing line, supplement line, the books, the training centers, all these things and now the acting is just fun. I mean that's just one more thing outside the box, like fighting, that I get the opportunity to do."

The Sylvester Stallone blockbuster *The Expendable*s, in which Couture played a former special-ops badass named Toll Road, was released in the summer of 2010, just two weeks before Couture stepped into the Octagon at UFC 118 in what was billed "UFC vs. Boxing" in a bout against James Toney.

Toney famously hounded UFC president Dana White for over a year about getting a fight in the UFC. He showed up uninvited to press conferences where he would heckle White, saying boxing was superior to mixed martial arts and he was there to prove it. With an impressive boxing record of 72 wins with just six losses, including some 44 knockouts inside the ring, Toney, even at age 42, was no slouch. Randy welcomed the challenge.

"*I hope I'm the first guy to get to fight Tony* [sic]," he tweeted after White finally capitulated and agreed to give Toney a fight. Even during prefight press appearances, some of which were attended by UFC legend BJ Penn and new lightweight champion Frankie Edgar, who were fighting in a title-rematch bout (Penn had lost the belt to Edgar earlier in the year) on the same card as Couture vs. Toney, White seemingly apologized for putting the fight together, calling it a "freak show event."

"It's a freak show," White told Luke Thomas on a radio show. "I said I'd never put on a freak show fight and I'm doing it. Listen, this guy [Toney] chased me around the country saying bad things about the sport. If he wants to get his ass whupped, I'm gonna let him. You want me to tell you, 'James Toney vs. Randy Couture is gonna be the greatest fight in the history of the sport?' No. I'm building a great card around this fight. You're not buying the James Toney vs. Randy Couture fight alone."

Couture submitted Toney with a head and arms choke after taking the boxer down with a high single-leg wrestling takedown, in the first round. In the end, it wasn't much of a fight, and Toney was sent on his merry way.

If MMA fans were worried about one of the heroes of the sport losing to a one-dimensional fighter, Couture hadn't seemed too worried. Just the day before his bout, when most fighters are focusing on their weight cut or getting in the zone for fight night, Couture was making autograph signing appearances at the UFC Fan Expo in Boston, alongside his son, Ryan. Randy wasn't worried about James Toney one bit. But it also illustrates the time commitments and the kind of responsibility it takes to be the Natural.

Between training and media appearances, fighting and autograph signings, it's hard to imagine Randy Couture having time to even sleep.

"Sometimes I'll get the printout of the month I just lived through, and I don't know how I did it. Most of the time I'm happy to pack my bag. I'm happy to go where I get to go and meet the people that I get to meet. It's one of the coolest things about my job. I get to see a lot of neat places and meet a lot of very interesting people, and I have a lot of fun doing it. Ultimately, it boils down to what I really want to do, which is get in the cage and fight. I want to compete, and I want to hang on to that as long as I rationally can and keep doing what I love to do."

But living the dream does take sacrifice.

> **❝**Obviously I've been divorced three times," he says. "It's been hard on my personal relationships for a lot of reasons; the sport in general and the travel and the training. You know, I don't get to spend as much time with my kids. I think my kids understand. They're old enough. Certainly, my little guy isn't but the other two, the adult children, they understand, and now my son is starting to fight. He gets it, but there were definitely choices made there and that's where most of the sacrifices lie. **❞**

What I've found in interviewing professional MMA fighters is that they've all left unfinished business in their athletic lives, usually somewhere on some wrestling mat. Some guys fell short of winning a state or collegiate title. And the most driven guys are the ones who lose in the finals by one point, usually because of something like a riding time point or some other formality that will haunt the fighter with those, "If only I shot for that takedown I was thinking about," or whatever, for years to come.

For Couture, it was his failure to make the Olympic wrestling team that drove him so hard and so far in MMA.

"I definitely think it worked out the way it's supposed to work out and I don't regret having not accomplished those things," he says. "Because I honestly believe I would have been satisfied. I would have been okay to retire athletically and just kind of keep coaching and doing the things that I was doing. And, I think those disappointments, those losses and not making the team, they created a burning fire in me to continue. And it happened to be transitioning to this sport. Fighting has been the same thing, and the ones that I've lost have almost been the most important ones to me."

In a sport where black eyes are common inside the cage, believe it or not, there aren't too many black eyes outside of it, save for a few positive steroids tests here and there. Unfortunately, Couture was involved in one of those rare black-eye moments when he announced he was vacating his heavyweight belt and quitting the UFC, citing a lack of respect from company executives (i.e. Dana White and Lorenzo Fertitta), non-parity in pay (he believed he was underpaid compared to other champions), and failing to receive a signing bonus he said he was promised when he came out of retirement in 2007 to defeat Tim Sylvia for the heavyweight belt.

Couture also made reference to the UFC failing to sign Fedor Emelianenko, who is widely considered to be the greatest heavyweight MMA fighter to have ever participated in the sport. A fight between Randy and Fedor had long been hoped for as a way to prove who the true pound-for-pound champion (at the time) was.

The UFC sued Couture for breach of contract, conspiracy to damage the company with unnamed competitors, divulging trade secrets, and disparaging the company. The company sought compensatory and punitive damages. A court then upheld a UFC imposed stay on Couture fighting for any other organization while still under contract with the UFC, and because of a "champion's clause" in all UFC contracts, Couture was bound for several years. He would have been prevented from fighting for a very long time had he not settled out of court and returned to the organization.

In the end, nobody won. Couture lost a year's worth of momentum and income, and the UFC had to have an interim belt match and pay huge sums of money in legal fees.

"I missed fighting," says Couture. "I realized my clock was ticking and I couldn't afford to sit on my hands for a lot longer, and they were going to try and drag it out as long as they could to keep me from fighting somewhere else. That's just the way it is. It's business. I don't think it's something I regret doing. I think ultimately, you know, the Fedor fight never happened, but I've still had a lot of great fights. I've got a new contract with them that is the best contract I've ever had. So, in the long run, I think it worked out."

Except for the Fedor fight, that is, which looks even less likely to happen now that Randy is making headway in Hollywood. Plus, ever since Fedor lost to Fabricio Werdum in 2010 via triangle choke, some of the myth about the big Russian being the best ever has begun to dissipate, and those conversations about a Fedor vs. Couture fight have been all but silenced.

"I feel like I had the ability to beat him. I see places where I think he could be exploited. I don't think he spent a lot of time on his back, although he has been there some. The rules of engagement could be telling. Are there elbows [allowed] or not? Is it in a ring or is it in a cage? Obviously, I think given the UFC rules in the cage, the unified rules in the cage, I have a good chance of beating him. There are some things to watch out for. He's got an unorthodox, very explosive striking style, and he's got a very good submission game that is not jiu-jitsu. It doesn't come from a lot of places where we're used to seeing the submissions come from so, I think those are things to be attentive to. But I think putting him on his back or finding a way to put him on the bottom, you know obviously that's where I tend to be strongest and how I would approach trying to beat him."

As of this writing however, Randy, and perhaps the entire MMA community, has moved on from the "Is Fedor the best" debate.

"I don't know that I need that fight as much as he does at this point. You know, again, I'm pretty happy and content and fighting down at 205 pounds, and there are a lot of interesting guys in the 205 pound weight class right now. I think because of the record of competition that he's had over the last couple years since this whole thing kind of took center stage has been a little more questionable than mine. And it's almost like he needs a fight like that more than I do at this point."

Randy, despite being one of the top-tier fighters in the sport when it comes to compensation, did receive a great deal of support from a lot of the lower-tier income fighters during his hiatus from fighting, because he brought to light the reality of what it means to be a fighter trying to make his way up the ladder. I ask Randy whether or not mixed martial arts would welcome a union.

"I think that there are still some holes, you know. Fighters as a whole don't have a lot of medical insurance and coverage. If [an injury] happens in the cage in that competition then we're going to be covered by the insurance that the promoter has to get to put on the show. But outside of that, they—and their families—aren't covered. If they get sick, if they get an infection, if they get anything, they're on their own. Even in training for that fight, before they get in the cage they aren't covered. So, there are still some holes there. I think there are still promoters that take advantage of fighters and don't pay them appropriately, or don't pay them at all. A lot of things like that still happen, so there is strength in numbers. It's a way for us to kind of unify and get a fair shake in a lot of ways. The actors did it; the Screen Actors Guild is the most closely related union activity that I can see that fits. There are a bunch of different promoters like there are a bunch of different movie studios and there is a whole slew of talent that can go to any one of those as long as they're part of SAG."

Of course, talking about unionizing and actually doing so are completely different continents.

> **"**I think there is an upside and a downside to everything," Randy says. "Those first guys that step up and push it through, they're going to get blackballed. They're going to have animosity from the promoters and all those sorts of things. I mean, it happened in every other sport where there was a union or players association or one of those things that formed. So, I don't think our sport is going to be any different. Those first guys are going to be swimming upstream for sure. **"**

Growing up a wrestler myself, the guys I looked up to were names like Gene Mills (Mean Gene The Pinning Machine), Bobby Weaver, Ed and Lou Banach, and Martucci and Yazou, each one of them about the same age as Couture is today. I asked Randy if he ever runs into those guys now, and if he is ever met with incredulity from his peers that he is still able to compete at such a high level.

"I haven't run into anybody on that particular list and my list is a little different because I spent that six years in the army. So, I would have been in that class of guys competing for those teams, but because of my time in the army it jumped me back six years. But, there are certainly guys that I run into that were in my class of wrestlers that are like, 'Dude, how are you still doing this? How are you training? I needed a hip replacement,' you know, all these things, and I'm like, 'I really don't know, I'm just having fun and getting better. It's silly.'"

On December 3, 2010, I went to Oregon State University to interview Chael Sonnen. The date is significant in that Sonnen spent the day in Sacramento at a hearing in front of the California State Athletic Commission to appeal his suspension for testing positive for performance-enhancing drugs following his heartbreaking loss to Anderson Silva at UFC 117 in Oakland. Sonnen would get his suspension cut in half to just six months, and I was there to get the first interview with him posthearing. The hearing was delayed, so I got to watch an amateur MMA event at the University's Gill Colesium while I waited for Chael to arrive.

This was just one day after I presented the International Fighter of the Year Award at the *Fighter's Only* Magazine World MMA Awards at the Palms Casino in Las Vegas, which Randy Couture co-hosted with Versus network's Molly Qerim.

As I sat in my seat watching the bouts, I noticed that between each fight OSU students bolted out of the bleachers and formed a line by the cage. I walked down to see what the commotion was all about, and there, posing for pictures and signing autographs in the gym, was none other than Randy Couture, back here at the place where he spent his post-army career years as the assistant wrestling coach and the strength and conditioning coach, before he left to pursue MMA full time.

There I was feeling a bit sorry for myself that I was bouncing from city to city, away from my family to do my job, and there was Couture, who made the same damn trip I made. The difference was Couture wasn't being paid to be there. Couture was there to show support to the school he loves and to the fighters who are competing in a sport he loves.

I walked up to Couture and we hugged hello.

I told him he did a good job at the awards show and he returned the compliment. We talked about the amateur fights we had just seen, and while he signed more autographs I talked to his beautiful girlfriend, whom I'd met the night before at the awards ceremony. We were all obviously dressed way down compared to the black-tie event just 24 hours earlier, and we all sort of looked at each other and laughed.

Without saying it out loud, we were thinking the same thing. We were thinking about how a little sport that brought us together 10 years earlier, was still bringing us together in Corvallis, Oregon, today. How a sport that was dead and buried over and over again back then is now a reason for a black-tie affair and a TV show—with both of us on it.

It was the reason I left an amazing job at FOX News Channel and Randy left a plum coaching gig at the school where we now stood. It was the reason we were both living our dreams and the reason new doors keep opening for both of us.

While I know my place in the sport is nothing compared to Couture's, it nearly brought me to tears to hear Randy say that I was one of the people who helped the sport move forward with media exposure when it needed it the most. I'm flattered beyond belief when he brings up interviews I did with him in the early days of the sport. Interviews he pointed to whenever people told him he was crazy for putting his time and energy into something called the Ultimate Fighting Championship. It blows my mind.

Because as much as I am a professional, I'm also a fan. And when my journalist hat is off and my fan hat is on, Randy Couture is and will always be one of my heroes. At 48, Couture is still one of the most dangerous fighters in the world, capable of beating anyone in the sport. Couture attributes his staying power to proper nutrition and the luxury of having one's hormone levels analyzed regularly.

"About three years ago I got my blood chemistry tested," he says. "This was in the middle of the UFC court case and all that stuff, so there was a lot of stress. I had a bald patch on my face, the hair was falling out from stress. It was not a happy time, and he tested my blood. He's like, 'I don't really know how you're even walking around. I mean, you're so far off the charts in your adrenals and all this other stuff I don't know how you can compete.' He started me on a supplement regimen through this company that doesn't do any public marketing, it's not fancy packaged, nothing like that. And within six months, all my hormone levels and everything came back into normal ranges where they should be, and I started feeling energetic again and I started to feel good and started to recover from workouts and just feel a lot more like myself. And I've been with that same routine now for the last three years and that same routine is what became the XCAP: The Xtreme Couture Athletic Performance Supplement Program. And a bunch of our athletes at Xtreme Couture have been blood tested and are using the supplements. It's amazing, all-natural stuff that has really made a huge difference for me. I feel younger. They can test the tail on the gene that tells your true age, not how many years you've been on the planet, but genetically how old you really are, and [according to those tests] I was about 32, 33. I was pretty happy about that."

Now that Couture had righted his physical system, I asked him how he addressed his mental and emotional system. After reading his book, *Becoming the Natural*, it was pretty clear that Couture had been dealing with a lot of relationship issues throughout most of his adult life. Now, at close to 50 years old, he's finally finding a peaceful middle ground with those relationships.

In his book, Randy was brutally honest about things that happened in his life. He was three times divorced by the time I interviewed him in the summer of 2010 for *Fighting Words*, and he was candid about being unfaithful to his wives. In fact, he cheated on his first wife with the woman who would become his second wife, and then cheated on her with the woman who would become his third wife. His mother was so upset by the way Couture's relationships continued to fall apart, especially when there were children involved, that she would not talk to her son for many months.

After the first season of *The Ultimate Fighter*, where Randy was a coach opposite Chuck Liddell, he got a call from a man named Wally Johnson, who claimed to be his father.

He called his "real" father, Ed—or who he thought was his real father—first.

> ❝'This guy is claiming he's my dad,' I said. 'Is this true?' My dad began to cry. Angry and upset all at once, Ed told me he had raised me like I was his son, then he stopped talking mid-sentence. 'Am I your son?' I asked, but my father would not answer. ❞

According to his book, Randy then laid into his mom over the phone.

"Where do you get off judging me and saying all these things about my divorce and treating me the way you have when you did the same thing?" he writes. "You've never told me the truth!"

He later writes that he finally got his mother to admit she was involved with Wally Johnson while she was temporarily separated from Ed, but still denied Wally was his father.

His mother was very upset with Randy for telling this story in his book, and his sisters were also angry at him for airing the family's dirty laundry in public.

I ask him how he handled that delicate family situation.

"I went to my sisters first with the rough drafts and got their perspective and their opinions because they, you know, they're my siblings. They lived and experienced a lot of the same things I did, and even their perception and the way they told those stories was different than how

I remembered them. But it was my book. It was how I told them. The biggest person that I think was disappointed and upset was my mother. And my mother has always been there for me. She's the motivating factor and the person in my life that was always there. So that was very difficult. She is the one person I never really wanted to disappoint, and I disappointed her several times," he says. "It definitely caused a strain in our relationship and it wasn't solely the book. There were other things going on too, but you know, there is some of that you can't take back. Again, I was trying to do something positive for me and positive for people that look up to fighting and look up to me as a fighter. I've gone through all kinds of stuff in my life and certainly it wasn't a tragedy. It was a pretty middle-class upbringing but a lot of hurdles just like everybody else, and I still managed, from a small town north of Seattle, to accomplish what I set out to accomplish. So I hoped telling people what I had been through would motivate them and make them feel like, 'Eh, my stuff isn't that bad, so I can do what I want to do too.'"

I follow up by asking Randy if he mended that relationship with his mother.

"My mom and I get along. There was a divorce and a small child that was…kind of caught up in that divorce too, and those, I think, [put even more strain] on the relationship. I mean, we get along fine now, but I don't know that it'll ever be the way it was, unfortunately."

In a way the development of his adult son, Ryan, entering Strikeforce as a professional MMA fighter, brings Randy full circle with his son. It's also a way for Ryan to understand just what his father was going through all those years when he was devoted to training and traveling so much. Ryan will experience a little bit of what it's like to be Randy Couture.

"I'm happy that he's a fighter because I see the passion in him. I see him in the gym. That's where he loves to be. He's a smart kid and a student of the game. He's learning to be well-rounded and that makes me happy. Not because it's the same thing I was doing. I almost think it's more of a burden to him than an advantage in a lot of ways. I mean, show me a guy that has his first amateur fight and he's got six people wanting to do media interviews with him. I mean, it just doesn't happen. He takes all that in stride. He learned through wrestling—because he wrestled through junior high and high school—kind of how to deal with this. I had accomplished a lot of things in the wrestling world, and now here he was trying in some ways to walk on the same path and so I learned to take a big step back. He had to kind of come to me. I wanted him to do this sport because he wanted to, and nothing to do with me or getting my attention or trying to please me, and I think that worked for him. It certainly worked for me. I get way more nervous watching him compete than I ever have while competing myself."

As of this writing, Ryan Couture is 1–0. He won his first professional bout via triangle choke; a move his dad had never finished a fight with during his entire career.

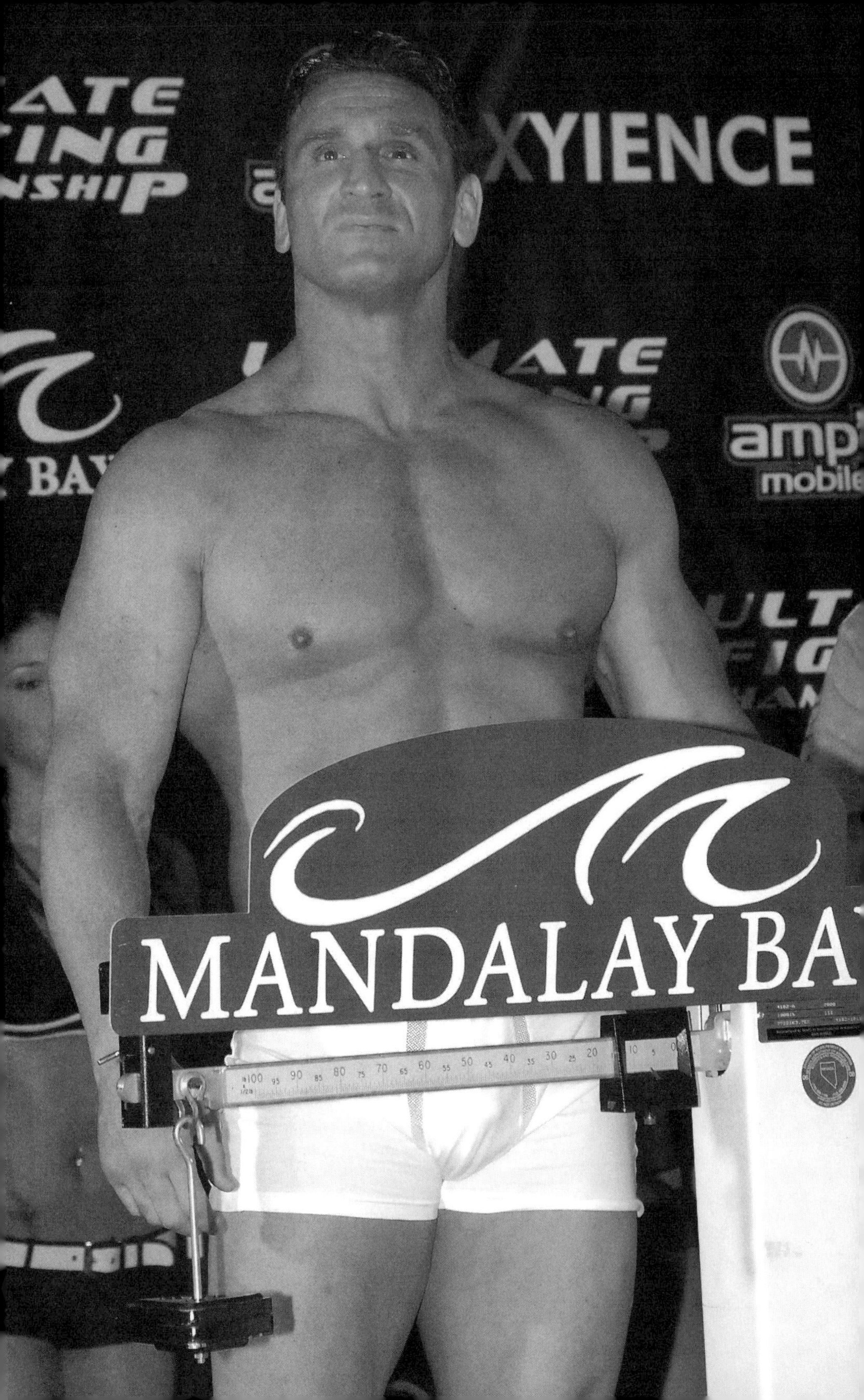
XYIENCE
MANDALAY

CHAPTER 12

KEN SHAMROCK, UFC HALL OF FAMER

What can I write about Ken Shamrock that hasn't already been written? He is an MMA legend, the first King of Pancrase, the first UFC heavyweight champion, the first man to ever put a beating on Royce Gracie (although their fight did end in a draw).

He is one of the first inductees into the UFC Hall of Fame. His rivalry with Tito Ortiz was epic, and the audience draws for each of their three fights set records at the time for attendance, television viewership, and total pay-per-view buys.

Ken is a huge star in mixed martial arts. He is also one of the most controversial figures in all of MMA.

When I interviewed Ken in May 2010 at the Mandalay Bay Resort in Las Vegas during the UFC Fan Expo, I was fully expecting to interview one of the most arrogant jerks to ever sit across from me. I braced myself for a confrontational showdown with a man whose reputation as a difficult person precedes him.

What I discovered was a vulnerable man who is seriously at odds with his reputation. He was hurt that, at the UFC Fan Expo, even as fans clamored for pictures and autographs, he didn't feel welcome. He felt that just by being there, he was doing something wrong. He was waiting for some imaginary ax to fall. I felt for the guy.

Ken was humble and extremely bright, as well as gracious and very thoughtful with his answers.

Our interview made headlines because Ken was honest about his thoughts about steroids in professional sports and even admitted to taking steroids. I didn't set out to have a gotcha moment with Ken. In fact, I agreed with everything he said about steroids and told him so. The fact that he had denied steroid use in the past, even after testing positive after a fight with Ross Clifton in 2009, is what the MMA blogosphere honed in on after our interview aired.

After we stopped rolling tape I personally apologized to Ken Shamrock, because I had been offered interviews with him for years, and each time I turned them down. I'd formed a negative opinion of the man before I ever got a chance to know him. I'd heard things like, "Ken Shamrock is a dick," or, "Ken Shamrock is as dumb as box of rocks."

He's not.

Now, where there's smoke there's fire, and I'm pretty confident Shamrock didn't get his bad reputation from nowhere. But if you're the kind of person who believes that everyone deserves a second chance, what I came away from this interview with is that if anyone deserves a second chance, it's Ken Shamrock.

For this chapter, I'm going to let the show transcript read word for word, so there's no confusion as to what was said. I'll let you draw whatever conclusions you will.

————

Mike Straka: Welcome to *Fighting Words*; I'm Mike Straka. Tonight's guest: UFC legend Ken Shamrock. Thanks for joining us.

Ken Shamrock: Thank you.

MS: Ken, do you feel like you get the respect you deserve from the UFC and the fans?

KS: Oh, you know, the fans, definitely. No matter what you do in sports, you're going to have people that like you and people that dislike you and I'm one of those people that you either like me or you dislike me. So there's really no in between there.

MS: So…are you okay with it?

KS: Oh, I'm absolutely okay with that. You know, I treat people the way that I would want to be treated. You know, if somebody rubs me wrong, I got to let them know it. I would want the same from somebody else if they didn't think I [was] treating them right or if I would have said something wrong to them. For them to say something to me, to say, 'You know what, I don't appreciate that.' That's the kind of person I am. That's the kind of way I want to be treated, and that's the way I treat other people. You are going to know what I'm thinking and I'm going to be respectful about it. But you better make sure you know that I do want respect because I give respect.

MS: Do you feel like you made the right decisions, career-wise?

KS: Hah, that's funny. It's funny that you say that because I don't think there's anybody in the history of sports that's ever made all the right decisions. So, no, I haven't made all the right decisions.

MS: You mean like Tiger Woods didn't make the right decisions?

KS: It's like, I think that Tiger Woods made several wrong decisions, you know what I'm saying? But you know what though, we all have that. I mean, we can look at a lot of athletes and point fingers and say, 'Oh he did this,' or, 'He did that.' And especially if you're a fan sitting on the outside looking in, because it's so easy to sit there and look and see what other people are doing when they're in the limelight, you know? But they—a lot of people don't realize what people go through when they're in those situations and what kinds of things they have to go through. A lot of people think it's just all fun and games. It's money, it's the high life, everybody wants to see you, it's the high road, you're living happy all the time. And it's completely the opposite. A lot of responsibility, and there is a lot of pressure. You know, 'boo-hoo,' you know what I mean? 'So what, you're still making all this money.' And it's true. It is a responsibility and if you are going to be in the limelight and you are going to be a professional athlete, you have a responsibility. And when you don't live up to that responsibility, then you deserve everything that comes your way through the media. You have to learn how to deal with that. Especially as a professional athlete, you better learn how to deal with it because it's gonna happen. And I've learned to deal with those things myself through my career. I've made bad decisions and bad choices. I'm the first to admit it. And that's what makes me able to recover from all those [bad decisions], is because I know when I make my bad decisions I will try to fix them.

MS: How old are you?

KS: Uh…I'm 22. (laughs)

MS: The reason that I ask is that you look amazing. You look like you're in great shape.

KS: Yeah, I know I feel great. I've been blessed to have the work ethic that I have. I train all the time. I have gyms and I'm working with different fighters in different places. You know I'm 46 years old and I feel very blessed to be where I'm at right now and [to] be able to still compete in this sport and have fun at it. And again, a lot of people stress on me competing in MMA—not the fans, because the fans want to see me fight again. But other people, and I don't understand why that is.

MS: What other people?

KS: You know, I mean, it's just different people and you know when you go into [naming] names, you start talking about different things, it's always a bad thing to do. *I learned that.* So the one thing I just know is that when an athlete gets to a point where, 'I'm not at the top. There's no way I'm up there in the top 10 as a fighter.' I know that, I'm not trying to relive my younger days. But what I am doing is having fun and living life how I want to live it and fighting people that I want to fight. So who am I hurting?

MS: And what is wrong with making a living? If somebody wants to pay you to fight, what is wrong with that?

KS: Well, that's just it. There is nothing wrong with it, but you know it's just rubbing a lot of people wrong. I don't know why they want me to disappear. They don't want to see me. They don't want me to be around. I don't know. I don't have any idea [why], you know. And I don't really care. My thing is that, there are fans out there that love to see me fight. And there are matchups out there that I think would be great for me to be able to have, go out and fight and do it on my own terms and have fun doing it. And that's what I'm doing right now. I'm not trying to take any spotlight from anybody. I'm not trying to fight past my prime and trying to be in the top 10. What I am doing? Like I said, I'm enjoying my life right now. I love life. I'm going to continue to love life. I'm going to appreciate my fans. It's something I've always done and I always continue to do and I'm going to do what I want to do when it comes to fighting.

MS: Let's talk about a guy your age, Randy Couture. He's a guy who has been fighting for a very long time, still at the top of his game. How do you think he maintains the level of competition he has?

KS: Well, I tell you, there are very few guys like Randy Couture. I mean, he's coming into the sport—I think he came in probably three or four years after I was in it. When he came onto the scene he struggled. He will be the first to tell you, boy, he struggled. But then he caught his second wind, you know. And then it was amazing to see what he did to

Chuck Liddell and what he did to Tito Ortiz. And then he continued to keep winning. I mean, the man has been blessed, you know. And you look at that and you got to give praise. What a great individual. What a person to represent the sport. He speaks well to people. He treats people well. That's the kind of people you want representing your sport.

MS: What happened that night in Florida when you were going to fight Kimbo? You cut your eye. Your own adopted brother says that you did it on purpose.

KS: (laughs) I'm sorry. First of all, I would like anybody—anybody—to try and cut their own eye. Tell me how you do that? Do it and stand there and go (makes a slicing motion toward his eye). Show me how that happens. I'm tough, but I ain't that tough. But this is ridiculous. You know anytime that you're in that situation and you have people that are hating on you—and that's what it is—somebody that doesn't have anything better to do with their time but to hate on somebody else, or otherwise, why would you say it? It [does nothing] but hurt somebody. Because if he really cared or really wanted something to happen or really was concerned about something, [he] wouldn't say things like that. That is directly something that was said just to hurt somebody else. That's all it was meant for.

MS: For you?

KS: Absolutely. I mean, why else would you say something like that, especially when you don't know? It's just something that was said because he wanted to hurt me.

MS: Why do you think he would hurt you?

KS: Dude, I don't know. You have to ask him that. I think there are a lot of reasons. A lot of insecurities with himself. Some of the things that he did to my dad. And I believe this honestly, my dad passed away and we called Frank up and I've always kept in contact with Frank, trying to keep this thing easy because I know how my dad felt. And uh, we have footage of this, because we were doing a documentary on my father and my father said that if he could get Frank to come, that he would put things behind him. And that he would like to be able to work these things out. And so, me and my wife tried to contact Frank, and we tried to get him to come in and he wouldn't. Then, my father passed away. We tried to get a hold of Frank and Frank's response was he was going to mourn at home. This is a man that took him out of prison. Gave him a second chance at life. Lived at my house upstairs in my room. I gave him a car, a Camaro with T-tops. I took care of this guy. And then he wanted to leave, that's fine, no problem there. But the way that he left and the way that he disrespected my father? Forget about me. I mean, I know I'm a hard guy to deal with sometimes. I know I have my faults, but my father has done nothing but help people and I tell you anybody you talk to will tell you that. And for him to do that to him, he's gonna have to live with that the rest of his life. And I'm sure he'll be okay with it because I know he'll kill his pain somehow.

MS: You were at the top of your game when you left the UFC and went to the WWE. Was that the right decision for you?

KS: Yes, and let me tell you the reason why—and most people don't know this. During those days when we were fighting three to four times in one night, we weren't making that much money. You know, I had four kids.

MS: What were you making back then? Like five grand a night, if that?

KS: Yeah, you know, I think max $30,000.

MS: For four fights in the same night?

KS: Yeah, I mean, it wasn't much. So you know, I mean, I was making ends meet, but I loved the sport and I wanted to stay in it. I was working over in Japan. I was doing stuff over there, so I was making ends meet. Well, then I lost my job in Japan because I was fighting in the UFC. They told me to quit. I told them no. I end up losing my job [with Pancrase].

MS: Who told you to quit, the Japanese?

KS: Yeah, you know, there were some people over there—again, I don't want to go into names because it will bite you in the butt when you do that. So I end up losing my job. And so, I stayed with the UFC. I fought through that.

MS: This was pre-Zuffa?

KS: Yeah, absolutely. This was Bob Meyrowitz in his days and Semiphore Entertainment Group, and they were struggling very, very badly. And so the prices were going down. They weren't getting much for purses. So I ended up losing a lot of things in that time. I started dropping off a lot of stuff. And so, I needed a place to go to where I could actually support my family, and I always said this, and I think I even said it on air one time, that I will continue to keep fighting in this business as long as I can support my family. And the minute I can't do that, I'll go do something else. And that time came. I couldn't support my family. So I had to go do something else. Those times were bad, and I think anybody can tell you those times were bad. We were getting thrown out of buildings the night before the shows and then loading up into an airplane 24 hours later and having to set up somewhere else in order to do the show. So it was really taking a toll on Bob Meyrowitz and them and they were losing a lot of money trying to fight this. And they ended up having to sell. And thank God the Ferttitas took it over and they brought it to where it's at today.

MS: Would you like to be an ambassador for UFC today?

KS: No. And it's not about the UFC. I'm not sure that you can actually put a tag on an ambassador. You know, you say, 'Oh, I'm going to be our ambassador.' I know they're doing it with some guys in UFC now. You see guys on drink bottles and you know, different things like that. You know they're forcing things down fans' throats like, 'This is our guy. This is the guy you're going to like. You're going like him. We're going to push it down your throat.' You can't do that. I guarantee you eventually that's going to bite them in the butt. The fans are going to like who they're going to like. The fans are going to respect who they're going to respect. That's the bottom line. You'll keep trying to do that and eventually it's going to kick you right back in the butt. So, for me, I don't want anybody to put a tag on me. I'll do whatever comes my way. Whatever God blesses me with, that's what I'll do. If it's an ambassador, then I'll do it. If it's something else, I'll do that. But I just don't want to force some sort of thing on me or thing on anybody else and say, 'Oh, you're the guy.' You know that'll happen. If it's to happen, it'll happen.

MS: Do you still come to all the fights?

KS: Um, I'm not, I don't know, I don't know if I'm welcome. I have no idea about that. I don't know. This is the first time I've been to a convention. I helped start this thing. I mean, it was crazy. This is the first time I've been to one. To me, I'm like, 'Wow,' I mean, did I make somebody that mad? I mean, I always thought this was a business. I never took it personal. You know, I always, you know, at times I did take it personal when it came to certain people, you know, I felt betrayed. But you know what, I put it behind me. You know, we're all kids growing up into a big world and sometimes we act like children. And I'm the first to admit it. I act like a child sometimes, you know, like I didn't get as big of piece of pie as he did. You know, whatever, you know, but at least I know that, and I can fix it later on down the road. But, you know, it's, you have to grow up some time. You know, this is a business and people are here and the people that helped this business get to where it's at, you don't cut 'em out because you're mad. How childish is that? You don't own the world. God does. Period. The minute you think you are, you're going to get stepped on like a bug.

MS: How has the fan reaction been at this event? Did they come to see you? Are they happy to see you?

KS: Um, you know what?

MS: Signing autographs? Taking pictures?

KS: Yeah, I think so, you know I mean? When I came here, me and my wife talked and you know, we were like, 'Wow, you know what man, this is kind of scary to go here, you know, and walk into this place when it almost feels like I'm not welcome.' And not by the fans, you know, and I'm not saying it's true either, because I really have never had anybody really come out and tell me, but just kind of the vibes that I got and I may be getting the wrong vibes, I could, I don't know. I just know it feels uncomfortable sometimes. But I've never been here before. I wasn't invited here this time. Um, I was invited here by Throwdown, um…geez I'm horrible. ("Combat," says Mrs. Shamrock off camera) What? Combat. So, Throwdown and Combat, they're the ones that brought me here and I so much appreciated that they did. But I was afraid. Because I thought coming here that I was going to, you know? I wasn't sure how people were going to take me because they're so many things that are done. You know, I haven't been in the UFC, I haven't been to the fights. I haven't been invited to places. I've just been kind of cut out of it. And, coming back it was like, 'Wow, you know what, I just hope the fans still understand that I do appreciate them and everything they've done for me.' And so, since I got here and I was doing the autographs and signing, it has been nothing but a pleasure. I thank God that, you know, all the times that I made sure— this is what my father told me—he told me this when I first started out, before I ever became this person that everybody wanted an autograph from—he told me, 'Make sure you're good to your fans, because they're the ones that are going to be beside you when you are done. They're the ones that are going to appreciate you when all your abilities and everything that you have are gone. They're the ones that are going to put you into a higher place. So you make sure you're good to them.' And I did. And I don't think there is ever one time in my career that I ever turned away anybody [asking for] an autograph—at least not on purpose. And I've always tried to be good to them. And I think where I was at today and signing autographs, my father was right. And I'm glad I listened to him. Because the fans do appreciate me and I appreciate them so much.

MS: More with Ken Shamrock. Don't go anywhere.

MS: Welcome back to *Fighting Words*, I'm Mike Straka at UFC Fan Expo 2 in Las Vegas, Nevada. UFC legend Ken Shamrock. First of all, welcome back. I'm sure as you stated earlier, the fans still do appreciate you. And your father taught you to be good to the fans.

KS: Yeah, that's one thing that he really instilled in me. And I thank God for that because um, there were times where I didn't want to do something because I was tired, I was training, or I said, 'You know what man, I just, I just don't got time right now.' And it just stuck in my mind like you know, 'These are the ones that are going to keep you up. These are the ones that are going to put you in a higher place.' That voice kept going in my head. So I made myself go to these things. And then when I got there, I was glad I did because anytime fans come up to you and they want your autograph and they tell you, and they're shaking, and they're so excited to see you. How special is that? I mean, do people really realize how special that is? For someone to come up and start shaking and hug you and just think you're the greatest thing in the world and all you do is fight? I mean, most people get arrested for that. These people are paying you and they're shaking and they're buying tickets to come watch you. Man, that is just (Ken starts to tear up) I'm sorry man, but if you don't realize that is a blessing, man, you got something wrong.

(I pause so Ken can compose himself)

MS: Ken Shamrock. First of all, let me say that for me this is a pleasure to finally get to sit down and talk to you and to get to really know you a little bit. I mean, what do you want to tell the fans about who you are today?

KS: Well it's not really [that] I want to tell the fans anything. I think the fans are going to make up their own ideas of who we are and what we are. Um, you know, we get to be able to be in front of the TV so much and the fans get to see this persona that we portray in the ring or that we portray in interviews. But who are we really? And the only way that fans really truly get to know that is really coming out and meeting us at autograph signings and different appearances. Because that's when you find out who those people really are, when they're tired, or when they're just being them for a long period of time, and that's something that I enjoy doing. I want people to know who I am. I'm not this guy that walks into the ring that has this stare across the ring that I burn a hole through you. That was a Ken Shamrock who went to work to be the best at what he could and I was not going to fail. I had this determination to win. It's the same thing when I meet people. I want people to know who I am. I truly do. I want them to know what I'm about. Because I think part of my being who I am and fighting has also been a blessing, but at that same time, I also have to let people know why I've had these opportunities and why I have been blessed with these things. And then I can share those and pass it on to them just by meeting them and talking to them.

MS: Do you think that people in the media, back when you were fighting, did they ever understand what you did? Because today, I think mainstream media does understand what a guy like Anderson Silva does or Randy Couture does. But back when you were doing it, did we really get it?

KS: Yeah, that was interesting because when people actually saw what we did, either one: they just went ecstatic, or two: they thought we should have been arrested. So, you really had a completely divided people who wanted it or people who didn't want it. Unfortunately for us, it was more people that really didn't want it. But they didn't get to know us, you know? I mean, they just got to see these guys go in the ring and just start beating on each other with no rules. And you know people were saying it was like cock fighting and, 'These guys aren't human, they're animals,' and you know it really, it hurt some of us because what we were thinking was like, 'They don't even know us. How could they say that about us?' I didn't understand why they were so angry at us. And the ones that were with us, were so fired up for it and so hungry for it. But, you know, after a while, when you start listening, you start opening up and you start going, 'You know what, I'm going to step back and I'm going to look at this and find out why it is that so many people are so angry at me.' You know, a lot of people loved it, but there were some that were really like just looking at me like I was crazy or something. I took a step back and looked at it from 30,000 feet up just to see. And you know what, I got it, you know? People that don't understand fighting, that don't understand combat. Even the ones that did boxing, when it hit the ground and guys were punching them on the ground and kicking them in the face on the ground, I got it, I got it, I understood it. And it was like I was able to deal with those people a little bit better because then I could understand how…what [they were afraid of was] kids watching stuff like that. I understood it. And I was able to deal with that better.

MS: And today?

KS: Today, I just think right now with the way the rules are and the way it's been rounded off where you have rounds and you have no kicking on the ground, no kneeing into the head, no punching in the back of the head—all these things that they put in there to make it safer for the fighters and at the same time make it TV friendly. You can block off a time so you can do a pay-per-view where the fights don't just keep going. You know, you block off a segment of time because you know how long the fights are going to go. So they made it TV friendly. They made it fan friendly and they made it safe. I'm absolutely for that. Absolutely, I think it had to do that or otherwise we wouldn't be where we're at today. So, I truly think that where it's at today, it's good. But I also think that the things that are going on in some of the places in the world of MMA is hurting it. And it's going to hurt it in the long run unless we change it.

MS: Like what?

KS: Well, for instance, you know there is a reality TV show, *The Ultimate Fighter*. Well, that concept, if you look back in, I believe it was '96, a book came out. The Lion's Den book [*Inside the Lion's Den*], the first one. And it talks about the fighter's house. The fun stuff that went on there, guys lighting people's hair on fire and, you know, burying them in you know, hold them down and shave them. There is all kinds of crazy stuff. Guys going out and getting drunk and coming home, all that stuff, right? Well, they took that and they made it into a show and I was like, 'Wow, this is great.' Well, at the same time too, it's not about how much TV time you can get. It's not about running through walls. It's not about how drunk you can get. You don't put alcohol in the fighter's house. That is a danger, man. Because I know if I was their age and I'm fighting and training and there is alcohol in there and I'm feeling a little bit bored, I'm going to the cupboard. But some of them kids have an alcohol problem. Oops. They don't check their background for that, so a lot of that stuff happens. You know? That concept was made for people to train hardcore. To get in there and train hardcore. To get in there and work hard. And it's now—and don't get me wrong because it's definitely interesting and it's getting good ratings so don't get me wrong that the show is not working, because it is. But that concept was for, to train hard. It's not to be—because if guys were drinking like that and partying like that, they got kicked out. There is no second chance. You're not taking the sport serious and you're not honoring the sport. They'd be gone.

So, I do like it [becasue] it is drawing viewership, but at the same time I also think that it could be bad for us in the long run. You know, look at boxing. I mean how many times did Mike Tyson go out there and knock somebody out? How many times did some boxers go out and get drunk and beat up their wives, and beat up their women and do these other things? You know, the same thing is starting to happen here. And we need to make sure that image that we're sending out to our young fans and to our MMA fans is that this is a sport that is respectable, and that we're not going to allow that kind of stuff to be going on. We're going to clean it up.

MS: Terrible segue but… (I laugh), and I don't mean this against Tito in any way. What do you think of Tito Ortiz now that he's back fighting in the UFC? As opposed to when he was fighting with you in those legendary bouts?

KS: You know, I'm not going to sit out here and judge someone's ability. When I came back—I will tell you this—when I came back from Japan and I came back into the UFC to fight, I knew that right then and there that the sport had completely changed. I mean here I am at 226 pounds, never had to cut weight before. I was always able to just go in and fight whoever, whatever, whatever size, whatever—and go in and do it. Well, now they had rounds. I had to come in, and they wanted me to fight Tito. I had to cut the weight. I never cut weight before. And I crashed, went down to 201 pounds. I tried to put the weight back on. I couldn't get it back on. So I end up fighting Tito at

201 pounds I think I weighed in at. Tito weighed in at 205 pounds. The next night he was 225. Right then and there I knew that the sport had changed. It changed and it was like, 'How in the world am I going to keep up with these guys?' You know, I just, am I just going to fight heavyweight? Um, I have to stay away from cutting this weight. I mean it completely changed everything with the weight cuts, the way these guys put weight back on. Um, it, it to me right then and there I was like okay, wake-up call. Maybe I need to stay at heavyweight.

MS: I look at a guy like Frankie Edgar who is a 155-pound champion at the moment. And he's one of the only natural '55-pounders in the game. Like you said, I've seen him weigh in at 155 and the next night guys he's fighting are back to 185, 190, 200. These guys are cutting up to 200. Yet this kid is like 158. But he still wins. I mean, God bless him. But you're right, I think that there is a weight issue. Do you think that maybe would it be different if we weighed in the day of the fight?

KS: Well, you know what, it's like this. There is nothing you can do to change that. It is what it is. That's our human nature. If you see everything that we are about as a human race it's always bigger and better. We're always going to make something bigger and better. We're going to find ways to do it better and bigger. It's like going to the moon. I mean, you go back early, way, way back when, and people said we're going to go to the moon, they thought you [were] crazy. Way, way back when we had wagons and stuff and they told you they're going to be cars driving. They thought you were crazy. Our human race is designed and built to get bigger and better in anything that we do. We will end up getting bigger and better ourselves out of this world.

MS: Do you think steroids should be legal?

KS: Absolutely. Absolutely. And the reason why I say that is because I think it's unfair when they just test the title fights. Because now what you're saying is, 'Oh, by the way, the guys that are making the most money, we're going to fine.' But how do you tell the young kids that are coming up from that, that you are setting a standard that you're not allowing steroids in this? You're not going to test 'em? Come on. These kids are hungry. These kids want to be champions. A lot of these kids are going to do what it takes to get there. Someone is going to get in their ear. They're going to see the results. They're going to keep going with it until they get to that point where now all of the sudden they're in contention and they're going to get tested. C'mon people, let's not be stupid, but we all know how to cheat.

MS: You know, there is a cliché in fighting [that] if you're not cheating, you're not trying.

KS: That's right.

MS: How easy is it to get steroids?

KS: (laughs) It's like going to the grocery store. It's that easy. It's that simple.

MS: But how easy is it to get quality steroids?

KS: Well, you know what, see, and that's one thing I think that you gotta ask somebody that really knows that kind of thing, you know [what] I mean? There is a lot of different stuff out there. I know that. But the quality of stuff or what kind of stuff is used for fighting and all that, you know, I don't know. But I'll tell you this, as the sport evolves, so does that.

MS: You know, I'm of the opinion that the guys who make these synthetic steroids will probably one day cure cancer. That's just my opinion. I don't think we should make it illegal. I really don't, because I think something good will come out of it. I really do. You look at what BALCO did, and the stuff that they made was incredible. Really, really incredible stuff, whether it was illegal in a sport or not, and I'm not condoning it for children or whatever, but…you know, there's gotta be something to be said for the amount of research and what they did.

KS: Well, you know, like you said, I think that steroids has a place in our society and in our life. But when you start trying to make things bigger and better, you're going to get yourself hurt.

MS: But what do the fans want? They want bigger and better.

KS: They want home runs, baby. They want people jacking them out of the park, but then when they find out about it they want to stick their head in the sand. 'Oh how bad, that was stupid, why did you do that? Are you crazy? Don't let him in the hall of fame.' It's like, 'Let's point the finger,' because if we don't point the finger at somebody else, we have to point it at ourselves, because we know. So, nobody wants to take responsibility but everybody wants to see it. And that's the way it's always going to be and it always will be. Someone is going to take the fall, period.

MS: Let's talk about, have you done steroids?

KS: Absolutely.

MS: Do you still do steroids?

KS: Nope.

MS: No?

KS: No.

MS: Do you think, obviously from the days you were competing till today, the quality of steroids has grown? And we hear about human growth hormone. You really didn't have that back in your day?

KS: No. And it wasn't that accessible, but you know, I know people on HGH who don't fight who just do it because it makes them feel good. Well, you know, there [are] age management programs out there, and like I said when I told you earlier on that there was a place for, and again, human growth hormones is not a steroid. It is a hormone. And there [are] places for that. And there is age management, which helps people who are older, in their sixties and seventies to be able to get their bodies to function like they're 40. So there is a place for that stuff that is effective and that is good for living. But again, like, human nature is that we find things that we can increase and get bigger and stronger and faster, and you know, the eagerness and the desire to be the best and to win is definitely very…[it's] overpowering being smart.

MS: Is Lasik surgery fair? Back in the day, Babe Ruth couldn't get his eyes fixed but today we can. [Is that, in a sense, like steroids?] I don't know, I'm just throwing stuff out there.

KS: Listen, you know what, you can argue all day long on that because everybody is going to have a stand on it. But I think what you have to look at is this. If you're going to go into a sport and you're going to compete, this is what I say. Everybody should be on the same playing field, period. Whatever that means, so be it. But don't you start separating things because you think that you've got to take it off the top and that you have to go off the guys that are more popular. If you're going to do it, then don't get prejudiced. Then you start from the bottom and you work your way up. And you get it out of all of it. Don't be segmenting it. Because you're never going to get it out.

MS: Okay, let's switch gears here. 'Ken Shamrock is a dick.' What do you say to that?

KS: I can be, absolutely, especially yes, my wife, especially when I'm six weeks out from a fight. (laughs) I get irritable. There is no doubt. I'm not perfect. And I'm the first to admit it, you know but there is one thing I can say though, is that I know it. And then when I do know it, I try to fix it.

> **MS:** What would you like to say to Dana White?
>
> **KS:** Um, I mean, there is really not much to say for me and Dana White. You know, I don't know. I guess I'm confused, really. I know there have been some issues and some different things that have been going on but to me it's like this thing has gotten so far out of whack. I'm not sure where it even [started], you know. I could, I could, I guess one place I would start just because I know the kind of person that I want to be and the kind of person I want to end up at, is, I'm sorry. If I've done anything outside of the business world, something personal, if I have offended you somehow or another, personally, I apologize [for] that. You know if it's business, I'm sorry, but that's business. You know this. We all know that we...I think one thing, you think another, and then if we both disagree, well then, we figure it out and we settle it, bam that's it. If it's personal, I'm sorry.

MS: Would you like to settle it?

KS: Dude, I don't want to be, I don't want to be in life and hate. I don't want that. I would rather go through life being friends with everybody and I know that's not possible. I know it's just life.

MS: But it's like you said earlier, we grow up. We make mistakes, we grow up. Would you ever just pick up the phone and call Dana and say, 'Listen, let's just talk it out.'?

KS: I have. I haven't said 'Let's talk it out.' I've just said, 'Hey dude, I'm sorry. I hope things work out after this and you know that we could be friends.' I'm always trying to keep that door open. Like I said, I'm not looking, and that's one thing I want him to know is, I ain't looking for no handout. I don't need a handout. I never did. I never want one. And as much as they want to think that I need them…You know, I do need them, but I don't need them the way they think I need them. I need them because this is who I am. This is my history. I'm a part of this and they can rip it away from me as much as they want. It's always going to be a part of me. I need this because I was a part of it, and I was a history of this, and it is who I am.

MS: What can you bring to MMA today outside of the cage Ken Shamrock? What is the ideal position for you? Would you like to be a commentator? Would you like to do what Frank is doing? Would you like to call fights? Would you like to be the color commentator? I mean, obviously you know the game better than anybody. What do you think you can bring to the sport? Because obviously, you're very well spoken. You know the sport. You seem pretty coherent to me. I mean, I've heard stories about you and every story I've heard about you, I can tell you right now, if anybody tells me right now, what they told me yesterday, I'd say that's bullshit. I interviewed him. He wasn't like that at all. So, what would you like to bring to the sport today?

KS: Well, I'm not sure that I can really bring anything to the sport. I think I've brought everything I can to the sport. But, um, if I wanted to add anything more to it, I would just like to be able to go out there and meet all the fans. I enjoy that. I like to go out and meet people. I want to meet the people who made me successful. If I had the last thing in my life to do is that I would want everybody that ever went to one of my fights and they enjoyed me fighting, that I could shake their hand and tell them thank you. And I mean that. I know you hear a lot of jumbo and you hear a lot of people trying to build their career and all these—dude I got my career. I don't need to build it. I'm saying this from my heart. I appreciate everybody who went to one of my fights.

CHAPTER 13

CLAY GUIDA, UFC FIGHTER

Clay Guida is one of those fighters who fans will love, win or lose, because he leaves everything—and I mean everything—inside the Octagon.

Over the course of his career Guida has fought top-level fighters such as Roger Huerta, Diego Sanchez, Takanori Gomi, Gilbert Melendez, Mac Danzig, Nate Diaz, Kenny Florian, Rafael dos Anjos, Tyson Griffin, Din Thomas, Josh Thomson, and on and on and on.

Clay is arguably the most prolific lightweight fighter in the world.

As of this writing, he has 39 professional MMA fights under his belt, and he's consistently brought a pace so fast and furious that his opponents are simply outworked time and time again. But, in spite of being an elite fighter, Clay Guida is one of the humblest men you'll ever meet, happy to be here on Earth, happy to be able to do what he loves for a living, happy to entertain the fans and happy to be in the UFC.

At UFC 125 I saw Guida walking with his headphones on, buried under a UFC hoodie as he was on a break from cutting weight on weigh-in day. Fans who recognized him stopped him and asked for an autograph. Now, at face value you might be thinking, "Well, yeah, that's what he should be doing."

Did I mention it was weigh-in day, where fighters are dehydrated, hungry, and generally ornery. The last thing they want to do is sign autographs. Clay did, and he acted like it was no big deal. He and I made eye contact and he knew what I was thinking, which was, "Damn bro, can't they wait until after a gallon of Pedialyte?"

But he nodded his head, saying, "It's all good, Mike."

Guida is often described by fans as the most exciting fighter in the history of the UFC, and while he won't totally agree with the statement, he tries to explain why the fans see it that way.

"You know, being one of the most exciting fighters, that's an honor considering the history of the UFC," he says. "That's excellent. People see the hair first of all, you know? They see the hairy chest, the caveman look, the Cro-Magnon forehead. But they see the big smile, too. They know I'm just out there having a good time, you know? My fights aren't pretty. People see me burp in between rounds, spitting, blowing snot, you name it. But it gets the job done sometimes, and being part of history I gotta say, I'm never satisfied with my victories or my losses."

Like Cain Velasquez, Guida attributes his work ethic and his die-hard attitude to the example his parents set for him growing up and said that he also tries to give the fight fans their money's worth every time he goes out to fight.

"My parents both worked a couple of jobs. So I learned hard work from them. I'm dedicated to my fans, too. No one wants to fight in front of an empty crowd. I'd rather not show up. I can feel the fans stomping their feet and clapping their hands as I'm doing my walkout, as I'm running around the cage beforehand and afterward, win or lose, when I'm in there it's like every punch I feel 10,000 fans behind me. That's what it's all about."

Guida is among other lighter-weight fighters such as Sam Stout, Frankie Edgar, Leonard Garcia, Urijah Faber, and Jose Aldo who seem to be able to fight forever after the bell rings, and fans and media often credit the lower-weight classes with being more exciting than some of the heavier weight classes.

"I wouldn't say we're better athletes. I think we just have less muscle mass to us. That makes us able to go. The action doesn't have to fuel our body as long. Um, and people ask me that, too—I'm sure they ask Frankie and all the other guys—'How are you in such good shape?' I tell them if you can't go hard for 15 or 25 minutes, you're in the wrong sport. And I don't like getting hit. It doesn't feel great, so no secret to it. Fifteen minutes is over like that, blink of an eye," he says, snapping his fingers.

In 2009 Guida was awarded the Fight of the Year award at the *Fighter's Only* magazine World MMA Awards for his bout against Diego Sanchez. It also made No. 13 on the *UFC Top 100 Fights* show and DVD. In the fight, which was broadcast live on SpikeTV during the *The Ultimate Fighter Season 9* finale, Guida weathered an early onslaught from Sanchez, including a vicious head kick that dropped the Carpenter, but didn't finish him. The bout was a back-and-forth slugfest that will go down in the UFC annals as one of the greatest.

"Like I said, I wasn't happy with the outcome," Guida says. "You know, split decision. I think Diego came out his strongest. He won three minutes of that fight. I've watched that fight over and over and I've turned the volume off. I've turned it up. I've listened to it, this and that. I've watched it by myself, with friends, with coaches. I think without the blood, I win that fight. The kick to the head, you know, people get dropped in fights but that first stanza where we exchanged, he landed like 40 punches; I landed like 25—there was a little blurb in *ESPN the Magazine* that my mom found, kind of cool. I think he won three minutes of that fight. I think I controlled the rest of the fight. I out-struck him. I took him down in the second and third round. But anyway, it's all water under the bridge."

Guida would go on to lose his next fight against Kenny Florian at UFC 107 in Memphis, Tennessee, and he said the back-to-back losses taught him a valuable lesson.

"If you look at those fights, I fought Diego's fight for the first round. I fought Kenny's fight in that fight, too. I fought my fight against Shannon Gugerty and every fight before that. And I'm fighting my fight against Rafael dos Anjos August 7th. When I fight Clay "the Carpenter" Guida-style, I get my hand raised."

Indeed, Guida broke dos Anjos' jaw and won via TKO (doctor's stoppage) in that fight at UFC 117. He would go on to submit Takanori "The Fireball Kid" Gomi at UFC 125 with a second-round guillotine, which was anything but expected, with Gomi coming off a one-punch knockout of Tyson Griffin.

But the comment about fighting his own fight reminded me of when I interviewed Bellator fighter—and former UFC star—Roger Huerta. Huerta was on a tear, fighting knock-down drag-out wars with the likes of Guida, Leonard Garcia, Doug Evans, and Alberto Crane. But, when he switched camps and started to training with Greg Jackson for his fight against Kenny Florian, he became a bit too conservative and game-planny, if you will, and he later came to believe that he should have stayed with what was working. Guida, who also trains with Jackson, had his own epic battle with Huerta in 2007. That fight, too, was a Fight of the Year candidate.

"Roger, he's a warrior," says Clay. "I think he and I are very similar in that our heart goes for days. He's probably a better athlete than I am, more skilled. Everything looks good when he throws his kicks, his punches and stuff, but he came back. I was winning that. One of the judges told me later that night after the fight I had him, you know? There was a 10–8 round—the second round—where he came out and knocked me into next year with that knee and stuff. I didn't even know which way was up. It's all heart. He knew he had one chance, and he landed it."

That's not to say that Greg Jackson ruined Huerta. In fact, if anything, Guida's wins against dos Anjos and Gomi are testament to what happens when one implements a game plan. Not to mention saving years on the end of his life by not simply standing toe-to-toe and banging.

Guida got his nickname, the Carpenter, after working as a union carpenter in Illinois while making his way up the ranks. But before building homes he worked as a crab trawler in Alaska's Bering Sea, catching Alaskan King Crab alongside Samoans who outweighed Guida by 200 pounds.

If you've ever watched the TV show *Deadliest Catch*, you're aware how hard a job working any fishing vessel can be, even tougher than being a UFC fighter, according to Clay.

"Hands down, being an Alaskan fisherman on the Bering Sea, it's crazy," says Clay. "I did that when I was 21, didn't know any better. I just wanted to travel the world and see different things. And I heard these guys were working hard and making good money and you know, I'm 21 years old. You think five grand a month is good money at 21. I blew it all partying, having a good time in the summer anyways—boating, concerts, everything. It was just more for the experience. But you know, I think every guy should try that at a younger age, get it out of your system. It's a good time. I wouldn't want to go back and do it again unless I had a family to support. You know, because a lot of these guys have been doing it for years for their families. I don't know how they can be away, you know. They have kids and things like that. I don't have any kids that I can be away from or whatever, so, it's just a great experience and it makes fighting seem like a walk in the park."

Guida grew up in Rockford, Illinois, near the Wisconsin border, the youngest of three children. He has an older sister who is a physical therapist and an older brother, Jason, who's a professional MMA fighter whom Clay credits for getting him into his current profession.

"He's the reason we're doing this interview right now. If it wasn't for him, I wouldn't have ever met you guys, you know? He called me one day on a whim, he's like, 'Hey, you want to fight tonight? Put down the beer and let's go.' You know? Some guy backed out. They needed someone to fill an exhibition fight. I went out there by complete accident. All I had was a college wrestling background and I went out there and choked the guy out and I got that burn inside me again where I wanted to compete."

In my field—broadcasting—people will say guys like me have "red-light fever," meaning once that red "recording" light goes on the camera, we turn it on. We can't get enough of that red light. For instance, if I need to replace a roof shingle on my house, it will take me all day to get up the courage to climb the ladder and actually get it done. However, if I were taping a segment on how to replace a roof shingle on my own HGTV show, I'd be done in one take.

It's similar for fighters, except instead of talking, they're getting punched in the face.

"People call us adrenaline junkies," Guida says, relating to my story. "I was just watching the X-Games the other day, some dude did a double backflip. Some guy tried a front flip on a dirt bike and almost broke his neck. Those guys are adrenaline junkies, and they think UFC fighters are crazy. I'm like, 'Dude, you just jumped a 200-foot gap and landed it. You could have broken every bone in your body. You guys are wild!' I look up to those guys. I just love competing. I love challenging myself. There is nothing better than someone saying you can't do that. 'Watch me,' you know? Just saying to yourself, 'I know I can get over that. I know I can go beat this guy. I'll grapple this guy.' I love testing myself every single day. There is nothing like it."

So what motivates Guida to want to get punched in the face for a living?

"It's more of *not* wanting to get punched in the face," says Clay, "to see how elusive I can be and see if I can take the guy down and avoid submissions. I love challenging myself every day and to me it's about getting up and being hungry every day. The day I stop challenging myself, the day I stop having fun in mixed martial arts and UFC is the day I hang up the gloves. I don't see that happening anytime soon, though."

Guida has long been a fan favorite—and for a few years that may have been good enough—but after finishing both dos Anjos and Gomi, Guida says he's ready to be the best of the best.

> **"**I want to fight whoever has the belt. Right now, it's Frankie Edgar. To me, BJ Penn is the most dominant lightweight fighter of all time. I look up to him. He's amazing at everything he does. Everything that guy touches turns to gold. I want to get in there and show my skills. If people want to see the best, most exciting lightweight fight ever, I'm going to be in it. It's going to be Fight of the Night. It's going to be Fight of the Year. **"**

Guida is best known for his UFC fights, but he's been around the MMA game since 2003, fighting in nearly a dozen promotions from Lemoore, California, to Juarez City, Mexico, to Tokyo, Japan. He was also the first Strikeforce lightweight champion before losing a split decision to current Strikeforce champ Gil Melendez in June 2006.

"I fought in the WEC before I got picked up by the UFC, back when they were in Lemoore, California, XFO, Monty Cox's production, Extreme Challenge, King of the Cage, I'd say close to probably a dozen promotions. I fought in Minnesota. I fought at Sturgis [Motorcycle Rally] one time with Kid Rock front row watching us."

Guida's signature trademark is his long, caveman-like hair that goes wild with every punch, kick, and takedown. It's also been known to get caked with blood, and he says taking postfight showers sometimes resembles something out of a horror movie, with pools of blood flowing down the drain. He also says the hair, while it works to distract his opponents, can end up working against him with the judges.

"It looks like it's in my way, but I've had it for 40 professional mixed martial arts fights, so I'm used to it," he says. "I think it goes against me with the judges—the guy might land a light jab and my hair goes flying and it looks like damage, or if I'm just moving my hair, you know I might slip a jab and I move the hair they might think it landed but at the same time, I can see my opponent planning what he's going to do, with the head movement and the hair in my eyes, so, the hair is here to stay."

Clay says the fans aren't shy about commenting about his hair either.

"I'll tell you what, I was at the national championship game [in 2010] and the Texas Longhorns and the Alabama Crimson Tide were playing. I went up and everybody grabbed their seat, had a beer, you know? This guy like two rows in front of me. He's like 'Hey, Guida.' I'm like, 'Hi, how you doing?' He said, 'I don't recognize you without seeing you in your own blood.' I'm like, 'Dude, that's not very nice,' and his buddy is like, 'You're an idiot, why would you say that?' But he's got a point, for sure. But I'll tell you what, out of almost 40 mixed martial arts fights, those are the only fights where I've actually been cut in, knock on wood, you know, I've been cut real bad in those two [Sanchez and Florian]. I bled like a horror film. People recognize those fights because they show them over and over. They're arguably in the top five lightweight [bouts] in the world, you know, so those are kind of etched in people's memory and one of them was Fight of the Year."

Like most of the fighters I interview on *Fighting Words*, I like to ask what their defining moment was, when they figured out, "Hey, I've finally made it." I love hearing about the moments where these men and women mentally turn the corner.

> **"**I remember a defining moment in my career when I was still working for the Chicago Carpenters' Union," Clay says. "I took a fight on a Wednesday for a Friday night tournament in Des Moines, Iowa, and I'd just fought Saturday in Chicago on another show that I held the lightweight title belt in. I just fought Saturday, having a good time, you know. I get a call and he's like, 'Hey, do you want to fight Friday in Des Moines? It's a four-man tournament. You get to pick your opponent and you can weigh 160 instead of 155.' So I get there, I'm the lightest out of all—they're all 170 pounds. I'm like, 'I thought this was a lightweight tournament?' Then they ended up sticking me with the hometown guy. So they didn't let me pick my opponent. I went out there, beat the crap out of this one guy, the home town guy, won that fight. Second fight I'm getting just thrown all over the cage by this kid Alonzo Martinez from Omaha, Nebraska, I believe. Beat me up. I hit him with the hardest right I think I've ever thrown and he does one of those (shakes his head), wipes it off, I'm like, 'Oh no, here we go.' All I knew was that I

double-legged him, speared him—kind of [WWE] Goldberg tackled him and the air went right out of him. You know you hear this, 'Eeeeh!' He gave up his back and I choked him out, and the whole place went nuts. First they were booing me because I beat their hometown guy, so it was almost kind of like a *Rocky* thing. I was losing and then came back and they were kind of cheering for me and that was like my 11th win, I think [Actually 12th]. And I'm like, 'I'm going to be good at this. I want to be good at this. I want to get that belt.'

"Then another defining moment was my UFC debut against Justin James on October 14th, 2006. I still remember it. I was on the undercard of Anderson Silva/Rich Franklin, their first fight. I went out there and he had me in this nasty arm bar, my stomach was done, and I thought he was going to break my elbow off, and I just stayed calm, because I was in that situation one time in Japan when I had lost when I tapped. I had to stay calm. I flipped around and ended up kneeing him in the side and the second round I came out and just took his back, choked him out and got Submission of the Night. I knew that this is where I belonged," he says, a smile spreading across his face.

I've always wondered how fighters know just how long they can stay in a bad situation before one of their limbs break and they're out for a year or more in recovery and rehab.

"You know what," Clay says, "I'm not too proud to [avoid] a broken arm, you know? I tap at practice. In a fight you let it go a little bit longer, and while I'm not the smartest guy, I'm not dumb enough to let an arm break or let a foot break or a knee or something like that. When that happens you're out six to eight months to a year, you know? So, if it happens, it happens. But I think sometimes in a fight, your arm, they give you a little extra bend and you might be a little bit more flexible because of the pressure, because of the heat, because of the lights and the cameras and stuff like that, so it's one of those things. I'm not one of those guys who's too proud to tap, because I gotta make money. I want to get in and have some more fun, you know? I don't want to be walking around in a sling when I could be at the gym training and getting ready for another fight."

Another favorite question of mine is, "When do you know that you've broken your opponent?" Guida smiles dastardly when I ask him, and I get the impression he lives for that moment. I bring up the Goldberg tackle and the "Eeeeh!" of his opponent in Des Moines as an example of him breaking someone.

"Correct," he says. "10 seconds later the fight was over. Remember when I fought against Shannon Gugerty? I heard him wince. [I'd been] skipping like a dozen elbows off this guy's head in the first and second round and he was just kind of weathering the storm. I didn't cut him or anything, you know? He was tough, but in the middle of the second round I just kind of felt him break. I squeezed that head-and-arm choke and he squeaked, and I just knew the fight was over.

> "Against Roger Huerta I kept taking him down repeatedly—and you could see it in his face after I watched the fight—but evidently I didn't break him. Against Mac Danzig I could just feel it. I saw him looking to his corner. I took him down, I saw him look in his corner, he did one of these with his hands (raises hand and shrugs in frustration), you know. It's very Randy Couture-esque. Randy is who I try and mold myself after a little bit, you know, one of the greatest champions of the sport."

Couture is one of the greatest strategists in the game, and in my opinion, uses the cage as a weapon better than anybody else in the game.

"Randy is one of the best fighters in his game plans," Guida agrees. "He knows how to switch his game plan on the fly in a fight. To me, that's what makes a true champion. If one thing is not working you have to have plan A, B, and C. He is also a world-renowned Greco Roman wrestler. I'm not. I never even made it out of state high school wrestling, but I always knew wrestling is what I was good at and what I enjoyed. We do a lot of drilling just up against the cage, you know, in the Octagon, and in the gym up against the wall mats, whatever it is, and it's just a feel."

Like Matt Hughes has said to me, Guida does not like cornering teammates, especially when big brother Jason is fighting.

"It's hard for me to watch my teammates, because there is nothing you can do. You're helpless. It's like your arms are tied. It's like you're in a bad dream. You can't run. You can't throw a punch. When I fight, we're cracking jokes, you know, as we're walking out to do our walk-out. You know, they're giving me water, I'm smiling at my coach. I'm smiling at my brother. I know this is what I'm here to do, I'm bouncing around like, 'Hey, give me another shot of water before this fight starts, you know.' I love it. It's natural for me. But, watching my brother and my teammates fight?" he says, shaking his head.

Speaking of Couture, who is 48, and as of this writing is scheduled to fight former UFC Light Heavyweight Champion Lyoto Machida in Toronto in April 2011, I wonder if Guida sees himself fighting well into his forties?

"Mixed martial arts is too premature of a sport to put an age limit or to put a cap on how many years you can be in it," he says. "You know, they say a running back in the NFL averages three to five years. Walter Payton, he played forever. Emmett Smith played forever. Injuries catch up to you. They say a defensive back can play for almost 10 years. I think an MMA fighter, if you train properly and fight properly, 20 years I think is, you know, it's reachable."

As my show is called *Fighting Words*, I ask Clay what pisses him off.

"People not being true to themselves. Simple enough. Go out there, have fun. Do something. Help someone out once a day, if you can. Say hi to someone. Shake hands with someone, a complete stranger. Just do something that makes you happy. And be true to yourself."

There's an obvious dichotomy there. How can a guy who beats the crap out of people for a living preach shaking hands with complete strangers?

"You know, it's kind of a double standard, but at the same time I'm always very respectful," he says. "I'm respectful toward my opponent, toward their camp—and afterward, too. But whatever happens out of that 15 minutes or however long it takes, there are no friends in there, but there is respect. To me that's what has brought this sport to the echelon [it's now at]. That is what has made the UFC the top organization in the world."

CHAPTER 14

RENZO GRACIE,
BRAZILIAN JIU-JITSU LEGEND

> **"**Believe it. Fighting is the best thing a man can have in his soul.**"**

That's Renzo Gracie (pronounced Hen-zoh) talking with reporter Scott Pelley on *60 Minutes*.

Pelley profiled the sport of mixed martial arts in 2006, and quite honestly, the piece still holds today. Back then most mainstream journalists looked to tear MMA down, and, as a former CBS News guy myself, I know for a fact that that was exactly what *60 Minutes* was intending to do.

But they underestimated their profile subjects, Pat Miletich and Renzo Gracie. They thought they would get stereotypical tough-guy bullies who use their martial arts tools to pound heads in this new "bloodsport" sweeping the nation.

Instead, what they learned was tradition and family values from Gracie and athleticism and hard work from Miletich. Both Gracie and Miletich have lives that span far beyond the Octagon, and they're both well-rounded and intelligent men. The result may not have been what the producers intended, but sometimes stories don't go along with the intended agenda.

Renzo Gracie doesn't need any introduction from me. If you're reading this book then you know who he is. You know about his upkick followed by a bare-fisted right to knock out Oleg Taktarov in MARS (Martial Arts Reality Superfighting), you know about his epic bout with BJ Penn in K1, the broken arm against Kazushi Sakuraba in Pride, and the guillotine finish of Pat Miletich in the IFL that was one of the anchors of that *60 Minutes* piece.

You probably also know that Renzo, at age 43, made his UFC debut against Matt Hughes at UFC 112 in Abu Dhabi in April 2010, losing by way of TKO with just 20 seconds left in the third round. Hughes crushed Renzo that night, and it was obvious that the Brazilian Jiu-Jitsu legend was a little too long in the tooth for the Octagon.

Backstage at the Ferrari World Arena, where the fight took place and where Renzo student Frankie Edgar beat BJ Penn to win the UFC lightweight belt, Renzo rested on the mat with his entire family. His wife, Christina, his daughters, Catarina and Cora, and his son, Ruran were all sprawled out on the mat at his side, as fighters of all shapes and sizes paid homage to the man they grew up idolizing as one of the pioneers of MMA. It was clear to observers—myself included—that no matter what just happened out there, Renzo Gracie was still a god to these fighters.

Frankie Edgar, having just won the biggest fight of his career, made a beeline to Renzo to show him the belt.

"Great fight," Renzo said. Frankie beamed.

At the postfight press conference (which Renzo didn't attend because he could barely walk after suffering devastating leg kicks from Hughes), I asked Hughes what it felt like to be the new "Gracie Killer," the nickname given to Sakuraba so many years ago after he defeated every Gracie who stood in front of him. Hughes was now the victor in bouts between Royce and Renzo Gracie. He also defeated Gracie team member Matt Serra and would go on to beat Renzo protégé Ricardo Almeida in the next few months.

"I like Renzo a lot," Hughes told me. "I have no beef with any of the Gracies, and I don't like that nickname. I'm not a killer. This is my job. It's not personal. In fact, I'm going to go see if Renzo wants to grab a beer after this is over."

To say that Renzo Gracie is a legend in mixed martial arts is really an understatement. Yes, Renzo has made a lot of money competing in MMA, and yes, he's won several world titles competing in jiu-jitsu, but he's so much more than that. Renzo's an author; he owns a jiu-jitsu academy with almost 10,000 members; he's been the subject of documentaries, as well as countless interviews for television, magazines, and websites; he's the Crown Prince of Abu Dhabi's jiu-jitsu instructor; and he's also raced horses in Dubai, a place where he famously won the Abu Dhabi Combat Club Tournament, one of the most prestigious grappling events in the world. Finally, he's a proud and loving father and husband.

He's trained and cornered some of the greatest fighters in the world, including Edgar, Serra, Almeida, Georges St-Pierre, and many, many more. His influence is especially felt on the East Coast, where his two schools are located, one in midtown Manhattan and one in Holmdel, New Jersey.

In my world I get to meet nearly every single famous MMA fighter under the sun, and Renzo Gracie is hands down one of the nicest people in all of MMA. He's generous, he's affable, and he's downright funny.

———

I ask Renzo about his UFC debut, and what it was like to lose in front of such a huge TV audience, and in front of the Sheikh in Abu Dhabi, his personal friend and now 10 percent owner of the UFC.

"I was limping for like a month but feeling great," Renzo says, adding he didn't regret not taking a so-called "tune-up" fight with a lesser fighter than Hughes for his first fight in more than two years.

> ❝No. I love it, and I learned a lot, you know. I learned that, first, you shouldn't let nobody kick you that much. (laughs) That's the first good lesson. It was important to see that, after two and a half years without training at all, that I was able to get in shape in six months. But, even though I could lose 40 pounds and I could get in there and fight, I didn't have the explosiveness and the ability to combine the takedowns and the striking. You know, it took a toll, so I got very tired in the fight. ❞

Renzo said he would need a full year of dedicated training and dieting and sparring before he would be ready to face another opponent in the Octagon, but stopped short of saying that his age played a factor.

"I've seen guys younger than me getting tired in the second round, first round. I took it all the way to the third round and was 20 seconds from the finish. If I knew it was 20 seconds, if I could hear my corner saying it was 20 seconds, I'd be walking around the cage, not letting him hit me." He says that the second leg kick Hughes landed did the most damage, and it was downhill from there.

"I couldn't move my leg well after that."

On Frankie Edgar's win that night, many of the MMA faithful questioned whether or not the Answer should have won a unanimous decision, and an immediate rematch with Penn was scheduled. Edgar won that second fight in even more dominant fashion at UFC 118, but for Renzo, he didn't think a rematch was necessary to determine if Frankie was a fluke champion.

"Some people question his victory like he didn't deserve to win. But, that fight was him a hundred percent, you know. He won it from the first to the last round."

Like being Dana White or Randy Couture, being Renzo Gracie is a full-time job. Between the schools, coaching fighters, training, appearances, and spending time with his family, sometimes it seems like too much for one man.

"It's very hectic. It's like, I sleep very little and I live everything to the fullest. But it's like, I do think lately I've been so busy and life, it's been a rush, so I have to be in 100 places at the same time. And if I could have a couple more Renzo Gracie clones, that would be better and easier."

With success comes sacrifice. And like many successful people, Renzo says it's his family and children who've sacrificed the most.

"I do think my kids and my wife [get robbed]," he says. "They are the ones who suffer most. But I do believe they understand that every break—every time I have—I'm with them. I live for them."

Randy Couture has mentioned to me that after so many years in the sport he's just now learning how to say no. I ask Renzo if he's learned that lesson yet.

"Yes," he says with a small laugh. "But in reality, no, I don't know how to say no. To me, it's always a struggle. I try to please everyone that is around me, and I try to make everyone around me shine and I try to push everyone forward, you know. I think this is one of my biggest qualities and one of my biggest problems, too."

It's these kinds of commitments that can hurt a fighter when it counts the most: in the fight. Perhaps Renzo's myriad obligations outside of the Octagon were a major part of the reason that he lost his UFC debut, which, despite Gracie's accomplishments in the sport, was a very important step for him.

"It takes a lot from my training. It takes a lot from being with my family. But, each person is a different universe, and I'm [built] in a way that I believe I can juggle and handle all of it, you know? Even though my last performance wasn't my best, I know it was preparatory for the future ones. I for sure will be better and ready for the next ones."

After the Hughes fight, standing in that outdoor arena in the middle of the desert, halfway across the world, Joe Rogan asked a tired and battered Renzo if he thinks he should have taken an easier fight for his first UFC showing. Renzo responded, "Then what kind of fighter would I be?" The crowd gave him a hearty applause, and Rogan complimented him as well. I ask Renzo to elaborate on that answer.

"I would be ashamed to do that," he says. "I could never do that. I would rather take a break of six months and train more to be ready to do it, than to take someone easier, or some tune-up fight to get myself back in the game. I'm glad it was Matt Hughes, and I'm honored to—if I have to lose, to have lost to a guy like that. It was a pleasure to share those moments with him."

I tip-toe around my next question. There's a fine line that has to be drawn between me and the fighters that I'm close to, like Renzo, Frankie, Ricardo, Serra, and so many others whom I call friends. I mean, Renzo's held my daughters and I've held Frankie's sons. At the same time, I have a job to do. Just like if I were a fighter and had to face those guys in the cage.

"Renzo, did you…When you were on the *Countdown* show or the *Prime Time* show, whatever it was, you were extremely relaxed. Um, very funny, very gregarious, um, it almost seemed like you weren't even getting ready for a fight."

> "To me, this is another day in the office," he says. "I don't know why people get nervous, why they can't sleep, they can't eat. They have to use the bathroom all the time. That's not my case, you know. I can eat, I can sleep, and I can use the bathroom on a regular basis like everybody else. I've seen everything. There is nothing that scares me. There is nobody that walks on two legs that is going to walk inside that cage that will scare me. This comes out when I'm walking into the cage and when I'm training, when I'm preparing myself to do it. It's not the boogey man in there.

I wonder if the loss to Hughes, which is perhaps the first time many new MMA fans have seen the legendary Renzo Gracie fight, might have damaged the Gracie brand? Does he feel the need to remind people of what he's done in the sport after such a high-profile loss?

"I don't really care. I say go try to walk my shoes. You have to understand how this sport was done by guys like me who had guts made of steel. So I don't care. Ignorance sometimes is a blessing. Let them be blessed."

In February 2007, Renzo fought on the first EliteXC card to be shown on Showtime (EliteXC is now defunct and Strikeforce acquired most of its contracted fighters), against the now retired Frank Shamrock.

Shamrock and Gracie had words before the fight, and the acrimony showed. It ended in a disqualification win for Gracie after Frank threw two illegal knees to the back of Gracie's head while he was on the mat, an obvious foul. The fact that Shamrock let his emotions take control to the point where he would throw the fight away in that manner shows just how much he genuinely disliked Renzo.

For Renzo though, what's past is past.

"I have no bad blood with nobody, you know. It's whatever happens in there, stays in there. And I do hope one day to have a chance to face him again. That, I think, is the part I like the most. Any bad blood we have, maybe one day we [go] inside the cage again."

Like Couture, one cannot think of the Renzo Gracie of today without bringing up the age factor. I ask him if the UFC should have a 40 and over Master's Division.

"I won't be in that division," Renzo says, a smile spreading across his face. "I'm not fighting guys over 40; let me tell you that. They're too old.

"But, Randy Couture's not an average [48]. He's a guy that people should mirror, because he's an unbelievable athlete. Very dedicated, you know. He works hard, and this shows you that a man is ageless. The moment he decides to work hard and push himself to the limit, age becomes just a factor in people's head. If you have the heart, you're ageless."

Renzo says guys like Couture, St-Pierre, and even Chuck Liddell will be great fighters forever, because they live like true white belts, eager to learn at every turn from anyone who may have something to teach.

> **❝**I see a guy like Randy Couture who improves every day. Like, every fight he does, he's better. He improves in jiu-jitsu. He improves his grappling. Recently I saw an interview about The Iceman, and he was talking about his improving jiu-jitsu and how he loves to train with a *gi*. This shows, a guy like Chuck Liddell who is constantly improving, there is no reason to retire him. Give him a little time and he'll be back strong as ever, because he has an open mind to learn and improve. Georges St-Pierre is a guy who is able to combine everything. He's constantly improving, constantly studying. He is the toughest guy in the Octagon because of his open mind and how foxy he is. He's able to embrace it and see things before they happen. You teach him a move, he stops and listens. So it's difficult to beat Georges St-Pierre. He will listen to a white belt telling him what to do. He has the patience to do it, which is going to take him a long way. You know, he's going to be a champion for a long, long time. **❞**

Since my show is called *Fighting Words*, I like to ask my guests what pisses them off, and most have the same answer.

"People who don't understand the beauty of this sport," answers Renzo, visibly bothered just thinking of them. "A lot of times I see this as ignorance. You know, they try to bash our sport. They try to put our sport down. When in reality, I feel sorry for them. They see our sport as something violent, something ignorant, and they question how beautiful and how efficient and how perfect our sport is. We have eyes to see the sport at a completely different level. But at the same time, they see it as an ugly sport. I see them as a bunch of figurative people who judge others, and they're just not happy with themselves. They have to try to put us down."

Being a Gracie means that you're a member of the First Family of Fighting, and that the responsibilities and expectations placed upon you are much greater than an average fighter.

Before Renzo's cousin Rolles Gracie made his UFC debut he was featured on the front page of practically every MMA website and did interviews on *FOX Fight Game, MMA Connected* in Canada, and countless MMA radio shows. Rolles would lose that fight to a last-minute replacement for his scheduled opponent in a fight that Renzo described as embarrassing. Another cousin, Roger Gracie, was greeted by a phalanx of reporters when he made his Strikeforce debut, and now Daniel Gracie (yet another cousin) has signed with Bellator. He's sure to be bombarded with media requests and expectations because he's a Gracie.

Renzo cornered for Roger Gracie in London in a bout against MMA veteran Kevin Randleman just a few months after his loss to Hughes. Roger submitted Randleman at 4:10 of the second round via rear-naked choke. Roger was awarded his black belt by Renzo, and he now holds a second degree and owns his own academy in West London, England. Seeing his young cousin win such a big fight, on Showtime no less, meant a lot to Renzo.

"Extremely proud," he says when I ask him how he felt about Roger's Strikeforce debut against such an accomplished mixed martial artist in Randleman. "He is an unbelievable fighter, a very dedicated kid, you know. He's a kid that I saw growing up and I actually—literally—changed his diapers, and to see him fighting and winning, it really fills my heart with pride. He's a very easygoing kid who has that unique ability of being calm in the ring. And I remember right before we walked out, I asked if he was nervous and he told me no. 'I'm extremely calm.' I was very proud of that. It's like the moment that you understand that's not a surprise box out there. That ring is your office and you're going to do it with passion. You're happy to walk in there and you're not nervous at all. So it filled me with pride, him being that way."

Despite all of the pressure it takes to be Renzo Gracie, I ask him if he's still having fun being the guy who is constantly being pulled in 10 different directions.

"I don't like it—I love it," he says. "I wouldn't rather be nobody else. Let me tell you that. I have a life that people can only have a dream of. You know, I could tell you 100 things that I did that people would sit down in awe, and I lived those. I experienced those. Believe it, they're going to have to die and be born again at least 10 times to have the life that I have. And it's all thanks to jiu-jitsu. What an amazing sport. It brought me to places and let me meet people and to live things that only jiu-jitsu could give me. The greatest gift my grandfather gave me was to embrace the art of jiu-jitsu as a way of life."

On the pressure of being a Gracie, Renzo is blunt.

"There is pressure of being alive. Life is pressure, you know, and I'm glad to be under pressure constantly. And if adding the Gracie name adds some extra pressure, I'm proud and happy to carry that pressure with me."

Perhaps the most famous Gracie is Royce, the first UFC champion and the man who proved to the world why Brazilian Jiu-Jitsu is such an important part of any combat sports arsenal.

Another famous Gracie is Cesar, the coach to Nick and Nate Diaz, Jake Shields, and Gilbert Melendez.

"Cesar is an unbelievable guy," says Renzo. "He is a product of mine, basically. I was the one who put him in jiu-jitsu. You know, I came to live in the United States for the first time when I was 18 years old and then, next thing I know, I drag him from Brazil to stay with me for a while. Then he got hooked up in jiu-jitsu, and today, look at the amazing array of fighters he was able to build. His model is my father's model. It's amazing. But everybody that came from my grandmother's womb, you know, they build unbelievable fighters. And Cesar is the living proof of that."

As a school owner and one who teaches a traditional—albeit modified form of martial art in Brazilian Jiu-Jitsu—I wonder if he thinks that mixed martial arts may, in some way, be destroying traditional martial arts forms?

> 66 No, it's not. It's actually reinforcing it. You know, you can't argue with the reality. Reality bites. Don't try now to say that you can karate-chop someone in the head and split his head in half—unless this happens inside the Octagon inside an MMA fight. That's the only way you can prove your martial art is strong, you know? We put our butts and faces on the line constantly to prove that. Because of this sport, now everybody knows what fighting is all about. It's the evolution of martial arts. You better be smart. A dumb fighter has a very short career. Muscles in this place takes you only so far, you know? You have to be a bruiser and a thinker. But better to be a thinker before being a bruiser. It makes your career last longer. The moment that he starts thinking and believing when everybody comes to him and say that he's the best, he's the king, there is nobody better than him, that's when he's done. He's gonna start fading. He has to understand that this sport evolves on a daily basis. You have to evolve every day. You have to improve every day. The moment that you see yourself as a master, you're done. You have to stay a true white belt forever. 99

Renzo said that he doesn't have a bucket list in fighting, but there is one thing he would like to see before he dies. This time, however, it's out of his control. The power to make this dream come true lies with his children.

"To see my grandkid fight," he says. "That's the only thing. Because I don't have a grandkid yet. I'm looking forward to that day, you know? I want to see him as a champ. Then I'll be happy."

CHAPTER 15

CHUCK LIDDELL,
UFC HALL OF FAMER

Chuck "The Iceman" Liddell retired from fighting at the end of 2010, bringing an end to a career that made him one of the most recognizable faces in the world, never mind mixed martial arts.

Liddell was the first real star of the Zuffa-era UFC. A five-time light heavyweight champion, Liddell propelled mixed martial arts into the mainstream conscience with historic Octagon battles against Randy Couture, Tito Ortiz, Rampage Jackson, and Wanderlei Silva.

Chuck finished his career with a professional MMA record of 21–8, with 13 knockouts, one submission, and just seven decisions.

Along the way, Liddell was featured on *Entourage*, was a character on *The Simpsons*, and even danced on national television on ABC's hit reality show *Dancing with the Stars*.

UFC president Dana White and CEO Lorenzo Fertitta made the joint announcement of Liddell's retirement during a prefight press conference for UFC 125 at the MGM Grand in Las Vegas. There the two also announced that Liddell would be taking on the role of UFC Executive Vice President of Business Development.

"He's now on level and on par with all the top executives," White said.

Liddell choked up more than once after he took the microphone to say goodbye to the fans and the MMA media who have followed his career over the last decade.

"Most of all I want to thank my fans and my family. I love this sport, and I'm excited to go to this new stage in my life and keep promoting the best sport in the world, the sport I love...now that I'm retired," he said.

Liddell was visibly emotional, and at times during his announcement he looked as if he was being forced to retire at gunpoint. A fighter to the very end, Liddell did not want to go quietly into that good night, and it was no secret that White, Liddell's former manager and best friend, wanted Chuck to retire dating back to UFC 97, when he was knocked out cold by Shogun Rua in front of 22,000 Canadians in Montreal's Bell Centre.

> ❝He's a huge superstar, and we could still sell lots of tickets [off Liddell]," White said at that night's postfight press conference. "But I don't care about that. I care about him. I care about his health, and it's over, man. It's over.❞

Liddell would go on to fight just once more since then, at UFC 115 against Rich Franklin. After coming out in arguably the best shape of his career, Liddell looked vintage as he stalked Franklin around the Octagon inside General Motors Place, even breaking Franklin's arm with a kick.

But just as the bell was about to ring to end the first round, Franklin caught Liddell with a counter left that knocked the Iceman out for the fourth time in his last six fights.

Liddell appeared on *Fighting Words* a few weeks before he officially retired, and one of the things Chuck requested I not ask him about was the subject of retirement. Of course, I respected his wishes, but I was able to get in a few questions on what he would do if he never fought again.

"You know, I don't know," he says. "It's when I don't think I can make a run at the title. It's one of those things. I still love fighting. I love being out there. I love training. I love doing it all, so you know, to keep doing it now at this point I need to feel I can make a legit run at the title to keep doing it."

From what I've heard from people close to Liddell, not even he knew what was in store for him until a few hours before White and Fertitta made the announcement about his new role as Executive VP of Business Development. Not even the UFC public relations staff knew what was coming. It was prescient then, that when I ask Chuck what could be next for him, he expresses a desire to stay on board with the UFC in some capacity.

"We'll see," he says. "You know, I'll still be around the sport, no matter what. And you know I might do some more movie stuff. I might do some more…some other things, I don't know. Spend some more time with my family, I think."

Liddell was a Division I wrestler at Cal-Poly and a former kick-boxer with an undefeated record before taking a mixed martial arts fight in the '90s. He made his UFC debut in 1998 at UFC 17, winning a unanimous decision against Mexico's Noe Hernandez.

"I did martial arts since I was a kid, and doing kickboxing was just something to keep competing when I was done wrestling," he says. "I was done wrestling. I wasn't good enough to go to the Olympics or anything, and I wanted to keep competing while I was finishing up school and kind of ran into kickboxing, so I started fighting. I fell in love with doing that. And then when someone offered me a mixed fight—he knew I'd wrestled in college and I was a kickboxer and he said, 'You want to fight?' I said, 'Sure, why not? I'll try it.' Just kind of fell in love with the sport."

Chuck says that he had an advantage in the early days of MMA, because he had two out of the three elements that make a successful fighter in mixed martial arts.

---

66 I think the thing for me was back then there were three elements you had to have: striking, wrestling, jiu-jitsu, and everybody came from one of them and was trying to add the other two and figure out how to put them together. And for me, I already had two. I had to add one and put it all together. So you know, I think I had a little advantage that way where I had a double background. Instead of having to learn two, I was just learning one. 99

Even though Liddell was a kickboxer, he's known for his one-punch knockout power. He was able to put people away from unorthodox positions, like fading back with an uppercut or simply counter-punching with a looping left. Chuck explains why he wasn't much of a kicker in MMA, even though he had a kickboxing background.

"When you add in the wrestling you have to throw a little less kicks," he says. Fighters who are good at takedowns will oftentimes take a leg or body kick from the opportunity in order to take them down. "But also, I had knee problems. I just kind of got away from kicking for a while. It's hard to get back. I kept hurting myself training, so it is hard. If you're not using it when you're training, you're not going to use it in a fight."

Liddell lost some pretty famous bouts, most notably against Rampage Jackson in Pride. Dana White agreed to let Chuck enter the tournament because fans were saying that Wanderlei Silva was the best light heavyweight in the world. However, Chuck lost to Jackson before he got a chance to get into the ring with Silva, and he lost again in a rematch with Jackson at UFC 71 in May 2007 by knockout.

He would eventually win a unanimous decision against Wanderlei at UFC 79. I ask Chuck what losses he'd like to get back.

"I mean, it's so hard to say. All my losses I'd like to have another shot at. But, you know, what are you going to do? With Franklin...

yeah, if it went a few more seconds he wouldn't have been able to answer the bell, so that's a tough one to take. I'd like to get back at it. I went out swinging the way I always do. I got caught. It happens."

Liddell is credited with helping the UFC gain national exposure, and his parts in *Dancing with the Stars* and *The Simpsons* were a big part of that, but an appearance on *Entourage*, at the height of the HBO series' popularity, cemented Liddell—and the UFC—as pop-culture icons.

"Yeah, I got a lot of people that didn't know me, didn't know fighting at all, know me now from that show," he says. "That's one of my favorite shows, so I was chasing people around saying, 'Hey, just get me on the show, I just want to walk on and say hi or something.' But they actually worked me into the script. It was great."

In the episode, titled "Gotcha," Liddell played himself appearing on a *Punk'd*-like show called *Gotcha!* hosted by comedian Pauly Shore, where Johnny Drama (Kevin Dillon) was duped into thinking he was going to have to fight Liddell in a charity event. It was one of the funniest episodes of the show, and of course became iconic among MMA fans—most of whom are also *Entourage* fans.

When I interviewed Liddell, we were in the Mandalay Bay Events Center during the annual Barrett-Jackson Custom Car Auction. A custom-made UFC Camaro was being auctioned off for the Intrepid Fallen Heroes Fund, a charity that provides support for the families of troops who were killed in action. The Camaro, which Liddell auctioned off himself, went for $350,000—well above what UFC brass was hoping to get for their favorite charity. (UFC Chief Marketing Officer Brian Johnston told me they were hoping to get anywhere above $100,000 for the car, and he said the entire Intrepid Fallen Heroes Fund was blown away by the gesture.)

"I think it's important for us to give back," Liddell says. "I mean, they [troops] allow us to do what we do here: live our lives here and not have to worry about anything.

———

Looking back on his career, Liddell was most satisfied with his wins over archrival Tito Ortiz and his biggest competitor during his prime, Randy Couture.

"Tito was the guy that was the trash talk back and forth," he says, which made for some spirited prefight hype, but for Chuck, Randy was the real deal. "The real competitive [matchup] was me and Randy. He beat me the first time; I knocked him out the second time. Everyone thought that was a fluke, and then it was nice to go back and knock him out a second time to prove it wasn't."

At UFC 118 Chuck's former rival, at 47 years of age, took out boxer James Toney in a mixed martial arts bout. Liddell wasn't the least bit surprised as to the outcome.

"It went exactly like I thought it was going to go. I mean, for all intents and purposes, it was over in the first what, five seconds? How long did it take him to take [Toney] down? Once he took him down, it was over. So, I mean, boxers, you can't make that transition without—especially those with no respect for the sport—if you're not going to learn how to wrestle or learn how to do jiu-jitsu, you're not going to last. A lucky punch with the guy maybe. One lucky punch is a chance, that's it."

Couture admitted that had he entered a boxing match with Toney the outcome would have likely gone the other way. Liddell agrees that fighters can't bounce between disciplines like that.

"They're two different sports; it's apples and oranges," he says. "I mean, your distance is different for boxing, for kickboxing. Remember when you used to be always, 'All the kickboxers weren't as good as the boxers,' because when the kickboxers came over to boxing, they got beat. Well, then when the boxers started going over to K1, most of them didn't do too well either."

Speaking of K1, Liddell is one of the only fighters to ever knock out Alistair Overeem, some seven years before the giant Dutchman won the K1 Grand Prix Championship Tournament on New Year's Eve 2010.

———

> **"**I knocked him out," Liddell says of Overeem, reenacting the punches he threw by shadowboxing as he describes the fight. "I caught him with a straight right. Stunned him a little bit and he just kind of shook it off. He did one of these things (shaking his head). Then I hit him with an overhand and he wobbled onto the ropes and I just...caught him. He's put on a lot of weight since then. I was shocked, but he's always been a good athlete. He was a good athlete back then when he was young. **"**

On Anderson Silva, whom Liddell has never fought, Liddell says that although the middleweight champion has one of the best stand-up games in the world, he has a glaring weakness that fighters, especially Chael Sonnen, are beginning to take advantage of.

"Well, I think he didn't make it difficult enough for Chael to take him down. Styles make fights. You know, Anderson Silva was dangerous every time he was on his feet. But he's got to make it a little harder for guys to take him down, especially if you know if the guys are going to stay and lay on him."

Liddell also has a long history with BJ Penn. The two have been friends for several years, and he said it was difficult for him to watch Penn lose his belt to Frankie Edgar.

"That's a hard one for me because BJ is my boy," he says. "First fight [UFC 112 in Abu Dhabi], I thought BJ won the fight, actually. The second fight hands down, I mean, he lost. So you know, Frankie Edgar is tough. He's giving BJ a hard time."

One thing Liddell has never really had to worry about was getting the respect from the MMA fans and media, something Edgar has struggled with throughout his career (although his draw against Maynard has certainly helped in that department). I ask Chuck what kind of advice he could give to guys like Edgar, who despite winning fights, are not winning over fans.

"Just keep fighting the way he fights," says Chuck. "Keep winning fights. You know, sooner or later people will come up and say, 'Okay, now you're good.'

Liddell said he typically competed two to three times a year and tried to keep his fights to five every two years. "It's a good amount of fights. You know, not trying to push it too hard."

But speaking of pushing too hard, one of the downsides to being a UFC star is the amount of obligations that come with the job. Back in Liddell's heyday, mixed martial arts was still a fringe sport, and there weren't too many demands on fighters outside of training.

These days there are autograph signings, appearances at Fan Expos, photo-ops, media appearances, and acting roles. It's gotten tougher to just be a fighter as the UFC and the sport of mixed martial arts has gained acceptance in the mainstream media.

"You know, you just get used to it over the years," says Liddell. "I've been doing this for a long time. I travel a lot. I'm used to going in and out of hotel rooms. But you know, that's part of it. I get paid a lot of money to do what I love for a living, so I can't complain."

Just how much money Liddell has made is not something I would ever ask; however, Canadian talk show host Michael Landsberg did ask Chuck what the most he's ever made for one fight was on a program called *Off The Record*.

"A couple million," said Chuck.

That's a far cry from the $30,000 Ken Shamrock said he made for fighting up to four times in one night.

On traveling and fulfilling those media obligations, Chuck says it gets hard to stay in top fighting condition when he's not around his base camp.

"Staying in shape on the road is hard," he says. "Because it's extra work. The biggest thing I lose when I travel a lot is taking care of myself as far as massages and icing. You kind of lose that in the travel time. That extra travel time always kills that spot. When I'm on the road I do bag work, so I just bring bag gloves and wraps. I don't usually plan on getting into big sparring session, outside of my gym."

His gym is The Pit, John Hackleman's mixed martial arts training center in Arroyo Grande, California. Formed in 1986 as a traditional karate school, it became world famous after Liddell won the UFC light heavyweight championship.

Hackleman was Liddell's trainer from the beginning to the end of the Iceman's illustrious career. That is becoming more and more rare in mixed martial arts, as guys such as Kenny Florian leave Mark de la Grotti and Jon Jones moves on from Team Bomb Squad. Using multiple trainers throughout a career is now more the norm than the exception.

"You know, John is the guy who got me where I was," Liddell says. "And we worked together for a long time. It's more like a family than anything. It's just one of those things [where, throughout] my career [this] is someone I've respected. And you know, if he told me I was doing something wrong, I figured I was, since he taught it to me. It made it real easy that way."

But loyalty is something Liddell is known for. As peers such as Couture and Ortiz split from the UFC in an attempt to get more favorable terms for their services, Liddell never had any sort of public rift with the organization he helped build.

"They've always treated me very well. Dana was my manager before they took over the UFC, we've been friends. And we've had our arguments about different things. It's just, you know, we were always able to settle it between us and figure it out."

Noted for his laid-back demeanor, the ability to work that stuff out peacefully may prove difficult for the newly retired Liddell. It's always been in training and fighting that the Iceman was able to exercise his more aggressive side.

———

> ❝I think that I get all that out in the gym or in the ring and for the rest of my life I'm pretty mellow and laid back," he says. "I get all my aggressive stuff out in the gym, so, it makes it easy to be mellow outside. I was just saying something to my girlfriend the other day, and she's like, 'You know, you seem to be snapping at people lately.' I'm like, 'Well, I haven't been sparring for a while, so maybe I should get back in the gym and start hitting people.'❞

Speaking of hitting people, one of Chuck's more famous media appearances happened on Sirius Radio's *Faction Rock Radio* show with Jason Ellis. Ellis asked Liddell to punch him as hard as he could in the arm, and Liddell dropped him with a solid right to the bicep, which in turn inspired thousands of young idiots to approach Liddell whenever they see him in public and ask him to punch them in the face.

"Yeah, I still get that one. That one is pretty funny. I think they're serious. I don't know. One of these times I should hit somebody and see what they do. I don't think they really understand how hard someone—a trained fighter—hits."

I tell Liddell that UFC fighters make it look easy. Much like when you're watching a basketball game on television, everyone is the same height, so you don't appreciate how tall those guys are until you're standing next to them. Chuck relates.

"I don't know how many times I've watched guys say, 'Oh man, that guy is horrible. I'll beat him.' I'm like, 'Wait a minute, I know that guy. I'll have him come by. You want to fight him? I'll fly him out, see how you do.'"

Liddell and Couture were the coaches on the first season of *The Ultimate Fighter*, the show that helped build the UFC into the juggernaut it is today. To put into perspective the impact that first season had on the sport, Forrest Griffin, Stephan Bonnar, Diego Sanchez, Kenny

Florian, Josh Koscheck, Mike Swick, Nate Quarry, Bobby Southworth, Chris Leben, Alex Shoenaur, and Alex Karelexis were all contestants. All of these guys have gone on to impressive careers, with Griffin becoming the light heavyweight champ, and Sanchez, Florian, and Koscheck all fighting for the title in their perspective weight classes.

When the show first aired, mixed martial arts fans and some fighters argued that a reality show was not the place to cultivate talent; however, Chuck says the results speak for themselves.

"I think [the show] has produced a lot of [good fighters]. You know, it's one of those things everyone always argues whether or not all these guys are getting in there the easy way. Well, even if they have an easy way in, they still gotta stay. They want to stay, they got to beat real guys. If you don't think these guys are real. Well, they'll prove it when they go back out there. [Season 11]'s Rich Antonito, they were saying that about him, 'Oh, he's got to go against a real up and comer,' and he went out there and beat the guy [Raphael "Sapo" Natal]. So, guess what? He's a real up and comer."

Liddell says he can see it in the eyes of his opponents when they just don't want to fight anymore, and recalls the time his kickboxing coach gave him the nickname *The Iceman.*

> **"**I think it was my third or fourth kickboxing fight. I was like 15th on the card, and I had to be there at 4:30, and I wasn't going to fight until 10:30," Chuck says. "Finally it was time to tape my hands and he was looking and couldn't find me. And everyone is looking all over the place and I was sleeping in a corner. And he was like, he'd never seen anyone, it was my 3rd or 4th fight and I was so calm, and so he started calling me 'Iceman.'**"**

One of the most asked questions Liddell hears is, "What does the tattoo on your head mean? And did it hurt?"

"It means temple of peace and prosperity," he says. "It's my original karate style, Koei-Kan, and no, it didn't hurt. There are no real nerves between the skin and the bone, so, the one in my arm hurt more."

While the UFC will continue to put on spectacular fights for years and years to come, Chuck Liddell will forever be remembered as one of the sport's greats. Just as Georges St-Pierre, Frankie Edgar, Cain Velasquez, Jon Jones, and Jose Aldo will inspire the future stars of mixed martial artists to enter the sport of the future, those stars of today will forever credit Chuck Liddell for inspiring them to don a pair of four-ounce gloves and step into the Octagon.

EPILOGUE

On Monday, March 14, 2011, the UFC announced that they had purchased Strikeforce for an undisclosed sum. The news broke two days before, in an interview with AOL's Ariel Helwani in Dana White's Las Vegas office, and it's pretty safe to say the development sent shockwaves throughout the MMA world.

The UFC was already the world's largest and most powerful MMA promotion, but with the acquisition of their strongest competitor they become the undisputed giant of the sport. The move, however, creates as many questions as it answers.

What does this mean for the fighters? Particularly, what does it mean for the Strikeforce fighters who've been expelled from the UFC, like Josh Barnett, Paul Daley, and Dan Henderson? What does it mean for Strikeforce commentator Frank Shamrock, who has called Dana White a bully, and is currently persona non grata with the world's largest MMA promotion? What does it mean for Strikeforce's founder, Scott Coker? Will Fedor now fight in the UFC? Will Showtime executives, many of whom despised Dana White after cantankerous negotiations had them flinging insults at one another in the press, suddenly play nice with the UFC?

I asked UFC CEO Lorenzo Fertitta on the press conference call announcing the acquisition if Coker had an equity stake in UFC; and the answer was no. Scott will draw a salary and continue to run Strikeforce as a separate entity within the company. Then, on Friday, March 18, I sat down and conducted an in-depth interview with Dana White after the UFC 128 weigh-ins in New Jersey's Prudential Center.

White went places he hadn't gone before with regard to the purchase of Strikeforce. He said Vadim Finkelstein, Fedor's manager, "Is probably kicking himself in the ass right now."

I asked him why.

"Because they should have been in the UFC," he said. "They should have come into the UFC when there was an opportunity for them to do it. Even if it was just for his legacy. If you are going to get beat, whether it's getting triangle choked or your face smashed, at least get it done by the best guys in the world. They probably don't care about legacy like I do, but I think legacy is important and for the last however many years, Fedor hasn't fought anybody."

I noted that if there's anyone on the planet who could fix Fedor's legacy, it's White.

"I don't think it's Fedor," White replied. "I've dealt with his management and it's 100% those guys. The problem is I don't think you are ever going to see a situation where Fedor is on his own and making his own decisions."

With the UFC's purchase of Strikeforce, Zuffa would be in a stronger place to negotiate with its television and Pay Per View partners, because it could now leverage Showtime's channel and its Pay Per View platform against them. For instance, if SpikeTV offered less money for *The Ultimate Fighter* than the UFC wanted, there could now be another outlet—Showtime—to shop its progamming to, creating a bidding war. At least that was my conjecture. White didn't agree.

"Let me tell you what's going on," White replied. "It makes me laugh sometimes when I'm cruising through the internet and I'm reading some of the stories that some of the reporters write and everything else. Nobody knows what we're doing. We know what's going on. We're the ones that built this industry. We're the trailblazers that are out there making all of these things happen. We know what we're doing and we know what the future is. We know what's going on and it's funny to sit around and read some of the ideas some of these websites throw out there. Trust me, we know exactly what we are doing for the next five years."

So how will the Showtime relationship work?

"Strikeforce has a deal with Showtime," he said. "That contract will be honored. And you know, as many people know who've been following the sport, I don't have too many fans over on that side of the fence. There's been a lot of things said, stuff that's happened, so, we're going to take this thing one day at a time. Lorenzo actually met with them yesterday, we'll send Lorenzo in there to smooth things out."

Was White willing to bury the hatchet with Ken Hershman?

"Yeah, absolutely," he said. "We'll see what happens when we all get into a room and start doing business. Can we do business together, yes or no? But my point is, we will honor the contract."

Of course, by acquiring its biggest competition, the UFC has left a vacuum where another competitor could come in to fill the void, and White didn't seem too concerned at the prospect of another competitor down the road.

"It's always going to happen," he said. "These guys aren't going to go away. The fight business is fun and we make it look easy. We make it look easy and they say, 'Look at those guys, they're making tons of money, we should be doing this. It's fun, let's get in the fight business.' You know how stupid that is? This is how dumb it is. It's like sitting on my couch at my house and we're hanging out watching NASCAR. 'Look at all the people there. Oh my God. Racing's fun. You know what we should do?' And then two and a half, three years later you're twenty, thirty, forty million in the whole, crying, looking to get out of the business."

Over the past few years, UFC has acquired World Extreme Cagefighting (WEC), Pride FC, and now Strikeforce. Together with the UFC fights, the company now has a vast archive of fight programming, so I asked him if he was looking to start a 24-hour UFC Channel?

"It's a different world out there right now," he said. "Going out and starting your own channel isn't as easy as it was six, seven years ago. But does it make sense? Yeah, it makes sense."

The irony of asking Dana if he was going to start his own channel is that a decade earlier the UFC was just getting back on Pay Per View, never mind television. I asked Dana if he felt proud of his accomplishments.

"Yeah, I'm proud of what the UFC has become and the things that we've accomplished," he said. "I never saw Strikeforce as a competitor. Am I pleased [about] all the organizations we've crushed before them? Absolutely. [But] the one who came out and wanted to fight, wanted to make a fight out of it? Absolutely. I'm 100% happy about that. But I'm actually happy to have Strikeforce and Scott Coker. I really like Scott Coker."

Like I wrote in the beginning of this book, I've been reporting on this sport since the beginning of the Dana White era. From day one, he was open and honest about where he wanted to take the sport of MMA, and the UFC. He said repeatedly that the UFC will be bigger than the NFL. A lot of people scoffed at the notion.

Ten years later, nobody's scoffing anymore. Congratulations Dana. And thank you for always making yourself available to me.

ACKNOWLEDGMENTS

This book would not have been possible were it not for the excellent crew at HDNet, starting with owner and chairman Mark Cuban, Andrew Simon—the CEO of HDNet Fights, president Guy Mezger, Executive Producer Darrell Ewalt, Adam Swift, Bo Vongsakoun, Kate Norris, Chris Taylor, Dustin Robinson, Donna Hutcheson, Matthew Gonzales, Jarrett Reichle, Todd Mueller, and Judy Arbogast, plus others I'm sure I'm forgetting to mention. If you're reading this book, you are a mixed martial arts fan, and if you are, you need to get HDNet. There is more MMA programming on HDNet than anywhere on television, from live fights including Dream and King of the Cage; *Inside MMA* with Kenny Rice and Bas Rutten; *The Voice VS*, Michael Schiavello's interview show; and my show, *Fighting Words*.

If there's one thing Mark Cuban has proven time and again it's that he's a visionary, so it's not surprising that he's the one media mogul who dove into the deep end when it came to MMA. A 2010 agreement with the UFC will only serve to make HDNet an even stronger player in the fight game, and with some of the industry's best talent that includes Michael "The Voice" Schiavello, Ron Kruck, Kenny, Bas, Frank Trigg, Jason "Mayhem" Miller, and Guy Mezger, it's only getting better. If your cable company doesn't move to carry HDNet, then find an alternative today.

Of course, the sport of mixed martial arts wouldn't exist, as we know it, without the hard work and dedication of UFC president Dana White, and the vast resources of Frank and Lorenzo Fertitta, who have worked tirelessly toward making mixed martial arts the fastest growing sport in the world.

Strikeforce's Scott Coker has furthered MMA with a television network deal on CBS thanks to his business savvy and hard work, and the faith of CBS EVP Kelly Kahl, who took the chance and who was the first to bring MMA to network television.

Bellator's Bjorn Rebney is doing his part to make professional fighting a reality for some great competitors with a tournament style promotion, and guys like Lou Neglia (Ring of Combat), Mark Pavelich (MFS), Rob Roveta (Showdown Fights), Monte Cox, M1Global, and others across the globe are working hard to provide a place for fighters to hone their crafts before hitting the big time.

I'd also like to thank my giant MMA family, who are far too many to name, but you all know who you are—fighters who trust me enough to sit across from me and bare their souls for the cameras, trainers who open their strategies to me, industry mainstays like Punkass and Skyskrape, Stitch Duran, Kenda Perez, and more, who show up at every fight and always have a handshake or a hug at the ready. And of course my fellow MMA journalists, whose respect and professionalism are part and parcel of why this sport has gotten so big so fast.

All of the public relations teams are instrumental for people like me, and I'd like to thank Jim Byrne, who after more than a decade of navigating media for the UFC, has been a stalwart in my life, as well as directors of PR Jen Wenk and Dave Sholler, Joe Fernandez, Strikeforce's Mike Afromowitz, Bellator's Sam Caplan, Showtime's Chris DeBlasio, and Annie Van Tourhout and Johnny Beyrooty, and so many other individual fighter publicists there are too many to mention.

Thanks to Mike Mcliesh from Head Rush Brand for making me a brand ambassador and getting me on *American Chopper* with Paul Teutul Sr. Mike understands the MMA business better than most.

Thanks to Jamie Salter and Perry Wolfman at Authentic Brands

Group for putting me in charge of media and entertainment for their growing stable of brands that include TapouT, Iron Star, Silver Star, and Marilyn Monroe. The crew at ABG: James Ling, Jim Gibb, Simon Chin, Noah Gelbart, Terri DiPaulo, Nancy Carlson, Anita Voss, Jeremy Castro, Julia Schwartzman, Matt Van Ekeren, Kevin Lauren Grosso, Barbara Katz, Dave Roberts, Corey Salter, Matty Salter, Kevin Clarke, Courtney White, Jordan Goodman, Paul Cohen, Judy Stonehill, and Luke and Charis Burrett, are my new family and I'm happy to be part of the team.

I'd also like to thank *FIGHT! Magazine*'s Donovan Craig and Jim Casey, Seth Kelly of *UFC Magazine*, Rob Hewitt of *Fighter's Only*, and Tom Gerbasi of UFC.com for giving me a platform for my columns, and a special thanks to incomparable Shawn Amos at the Amos Content Group and Shari Spencer at the Spencer Firm. Shawn keeps me busy blogging on the sport for clients like Spike.com, and Shari was the little birdie in Andrew Simon and Adam Swift's ears when HDNet was looking for another MMA host.

When I hosted and executive-produced *FOX Fight Game* at FOX News Channel, where I was also Vice President and Executive Producer of digital video, I worked with incredibly talented and passionate people like Jason Ehrich and Matt Riggs, a great studio crew led by Benny Almonte, and directors Jack Hanick and Frank Scudero. I also had a great panel in Frankie Edgar, Ariel Helwani, Peter Storm, Marcus Mera, Danielle Schatz, Alison Haislip, comedian Robert Kelly, John Moody, Andrew Falzone, Holly Madison, Donovan Craig, Larry Pepe, Josh Gross, Courtney Friel, and many more.

I'd also like to thank my freelance camera man Rick Smosky for being a steady hand (and eye) behind the camera, always giving me the confidence to get through a tough stand-up or interview, and *Fight Game* would never have been as big or as good as it was without the support of people like Derek Cifrodelli, Jason Ehrich, Dave Brown, and Gavin Hadden, who were the only ones who truly believed in what I was doing.

The biggest thanks, however, goes to my trusty editor/producer/shooter Justin Craig, who traveled with me to every event from Las

796.6

OCT 26 2011

JAN 23 2012

Vegas to Cologne, Germany, shooting and editing and uploading clips faster than anyone else in the business. Thanks for generally making me look good all of those years with excellent graphics, excellent story composition, and music mixing, and more than once cutting out a stupid question, an asinine mistake, or a general flub on my part to keep the boss honest with the viewers. I miss you, Justin, and I look forward to the day we will work together again.

Thanks to my literary agent, Ian Kleinert, who would be the greatest cage fighter in the world if only he would just train a little (and put on about 100 pounds), and my broadcast agents at Octagon Entertainment: John Ferriter and Kyell Thomas.

And to MMA-film directing legend Bobby Razak for his continued support of all things Mike Straka and TapouT! Thanks man.

Thanks to everybody at Triumph Books for believing in MMA and producing books that help proliferate the sport, and this book wouldn't have been possible without Tom Bast, Jesse Jordan, Paul Petrowsky, and Natalie King.

Thanks to my friend and UFC legend Randy Couture for writing the foreword to this book, and for being such a great ambassador for MMA.

I want to give a shout-out to my parents Frank and Elizabeth Straka, who are still my No. 1 fans, my nephews Greg English and Miles Straw—two budding jiu-jitsu players, my sister Melissa and brother-in-law Joe, as well as my in-laws Jack and Ann Straw, whose great taste in fine wine makes Christmas and Thanksgiving that much more special. A shout-out to my niece Ali and nephew Evan, and to my long lost nephew Cal Moseman, a Navy sailor stationed in Iraq, I want to say welcome to the family. We are so proud of you and I speak for your entire extended Straka family when I say we all feel utterly robbed that it took 21 years to finally get the chance to open our hearts to you. Finally, to my wife Emily, who puts up with my travel schedule and everything that entails, and takes care of my girls, Maxine and Olive, better than I ever could. Thank you for always being here for all of us.